SEVEN WORDS
OF
LOVE

Other books by Herbert Lockyer

All the Men of the Bible
All the Women of the Bible
All the Miracles of the Bible
All the Parables of the Bible
All the Doctrines of the Bible
All the Kings and Queens of the Bible
All the Children of the Bible
All the Prayers of the Bible
All the Promises of the Bible
All the Books and Chapters of the Bible
All the Holy Days and Holidays
All the Trades and Occupations of the Bible
All the Apostles of the Bible
All the Messianic Prophecies of the Bible
The Funeral Sourcebook
The Lenten Sourcebook
The Man Who Changed the World (2 vols.)
The Week That Changed the World
Last Words of Saints and Sinners
The Sins of Saints
The Gospel of the Life Beyond
The Unseen Army
Twin Truths of Scripture (2 vols.)
Triple Truths of Scripture (3 vols.)

HERBERT LOCKYER

SEVEN WORDS OF LOVE

Word Books, Publisher
Waco, Texas

To Him
by
whose stripes
I
am healed

CONTENTS

FOREWORD

The undying phrases that fell from the parched lips of Jesus as He died upon the cross have ever been a fertile field of exposition by preachers, especially during the Easter season, and because they are quite inexhaustible can be approached in so many different ways. In the *Introduction* of his classic in religious literature on these last sayings, *Christ's Words from the Cross*, C. H. Spurgeon says they are

> Like the steps of a ladder or the links of a golden chain, there is a mutual dependence and interlinking of each of the *Cries*, so that one leads to another and that to a third. Separately or in connection, our Master's words overflow with instruction to thoughtful minds.

This remarkable expositor of Scripture, who earned the accolade of "The Prince of Preachers," also reminds us that because these Seven Sayings were so faithfully recorded, it is no wonder that they have frequently been the subject of devout meditation:

> Fathers and confessors, preachers and divines have delighted to dwell upon every syllable of these matchless Cries. These solemn sentences have shone like the seven golden candlesticks or the seven stars of the Apocalypse, and have lighted multitudes of men to Him Who spake them. Thoughtful men have drawn a wealth of meaning from them, and in so doing have arranged them into different groups, and placed them under several heads.

9

It is most profitable to study the many volumes dealing specifically with these Last Sayings and note the different ways by which different minds approach them. Dr. Hubert Simpson in his *Testament of Love* says that

> The Seven Words uttered on the Cross are *seven windows* through which we may gaze at Christ. They have a sevenfold completeness. He died as He had lived. There is order and progress in those seven utterances. All through life Jesus had thought of His enemies first and of Himself last. In the pains of death it is the same.

Dr. S. J. Reid calls his exposition of these Seven Last Words of Jesus, *The Seven Windows,* and then develops his treatment of them in this interesting fashion:

> The First Window: Father, forgive them; for they know not what they do . . .
> The Second Window: Today shalt thou be with me in paradise.
> The Third Window: Woman, behold thy Son . . . behold thy mother!
> The Fourth Window: My God, my God, why hast thou forsaken me?
> The Fifth Window: I thirst.
> The Sixth Window: It is finished.
> The Seventh Window: Father, into thy hands I commend my spirit.

It is impossible this side of eternity to exhaust all the lessons to be learned from the Savior's sufferings and sayings as He died upon the cross for our redemption. What rays of holiness, grace, and wisdom they reflect! Further, with their tenderness, tragedy, and triumph they are incomparable. As Neil M. Fraser expresses it in his appealing study *The Grandeur of Golgotha:*

> The perfect ministry of the Cross, in terms of Divine communications, is seen in seven utterances of our Lord. At a time when other sufferers might excusably have given to morbid introspection and self-pity, these cries exhibit a breadth

of interest, a depth of consecration, and a vigour of utterance
that is profound because God-breathed. Here are no waning
of His powers, whether mental or physical. His last cries will
not be in the nature of a parting sigh which we sometimes
sing about and deplore that none were there to share it, but
spoken in a *loud voice* that Heaven as well as Earth, and Hell
as well as Heaven, might hear.

St. Bernard, whose heart loved the crucified Savior, and
whose lips and pen extolled His death, described His last
words from the cross as "The seven living leaves put forth
by our Vine." And taken as a whole, they fittingly summarize the person and offices of our Lord and the tenets of
the faith He caused to be "once delivered unto saints."

As seen from the references which follow, one saying is
given by Matthew and Mark conjointly, three by Luke, and
three by John. All seven of the sayings fall into two groups;
the first three into one group and the last four into another.
Three words were spoken to God, the Father; and four to
those close to Jesus. Three and four make seven, the sacred
number of Scripture indicating completeness or perfection.
The first three utterances present the three great branches
of Christ's mediatorial work.

THE FIRST WORD, Luke 23:34

Christ's ministry on the cross began with the forgiveness
of sin—with a plea for forgiveness, full and free, for a world
of sinners lost, and ruined by the Fall. In His prayer, "Father,
forgive them," the suffering One revealed Himself as the
interceding mediator pleading for the guilty. He lived
praying for others, and died doing the same. An aspect of
our holy faith is that such an efficacious ministry has never
ceased for He ever lives to make intercession for those redeemed by His precious blood.

THE SECOND WORD, Luke 23:43

The immediate response of Christ to the plea of the dying
thief, who accepted his companion in suffering as his personal Savior was, "Today shalt thou be with me in paradise."
Together in pain, they were to be together in Paradise.

"Lord, remember me," was rewarded by instant admission into the realms of eternal bliss. The man who died to sin on his cross, through the Man on the middle cross, departed with Christ, to be with Him forever. By this act Christ revealed His kingly power to open the gate of heaven for a poor, contrite sinner to enter. The Bible knows of no purgatory after death. All who die in Christ find themselves instantly with Him in Glory.

THE THIRD WORD, John 19:26, 27

Although He died as "The Prince of Glory," the true and proper humanity of Christ is emphasized in the recognition of His human relationship to Mary, whose first child He was. While He honored His mother, He did not worship her. Dying in agony, Jesus saw His mother standing by the cross and thought of her grief and need. Truly born of a woman, He opened a future, loving home for Mary and thus committed her to John's care. "Behold thy mother!" As He had opened paradise to a repentant robber, He now opens a permanent abode for His mother.

THE FOURTH WORD, Matthew 27:46

This further cry from the cross reminds us how deep were the waters crossed before the smitten Shepherd found the sheep that was lost. Forsaken of His God indicates something of the penalty Jesus endured as He died, the sinless substitute for sinners. The withdrawing of Jehovah's face, not from His well-beloved Son, but from the load of iniquity He carried, caused His human *soul* deep anguish and perplexity. God is of "purer eyes than to behold evil, and canst not look on iniquity," Habakkuk 1:13. Martin Luther says of this fourth cry, "Here we have God forsaken of God."

THE FIFTH WORD, John 19:28

This "cry of the human" was the fulfillment of a Scripture written a thousand years before Jesus cried, "I thirst!" As a partaker of our flesh and blood, Jesus experienced the agony of liquid to wet His fevered lips. Keeping His Godhead in reserve, He entered into the full sorrows of humanity. In all points He was touched with the feeling of our infirmities, and His mortal flesh shared in the anguish of His inward spirit. John says that Scripture was fulfilled by this cry, and thus confirms the fact that every word and act of Jesus, as the Living Word, confirmed the divine veracity of the written Word.

> In every pang that rends the heart
> The Man of Sorrows has a part.

THE SIXTH WORD, John 19:30

Is there not a thrill of victory in the tones of the announcement, "It is finished," which is only one lengthy word in the original Greek language? This was not the cry of a victim, but the shout of a victor. Now complete justification is ours seeing Jesus put away sin by the sacrifice of Himself. By His death and resurrection He made an end of sin and brought in everlasting righteousness and will ever remain as the Captain of our salvation. The old divines loved to speak of "the finished work of Calvary."

THE SEVENTH WORD, Luke 23:46

Three of the seven sayings were actually *prayers*—the first, fourth, and seventh sayings were addressed to God the Father. As the last of these final words of Jesus was also taken from the Old Testament, we have an insight into His source of comfort as He bowed His head and died. This last expiring word, "Father, into thy hands I commend my spirit," is the note of acceptance for Himself and for us all. As He commends His spirit into the Father's hands, so He brings all believers near to God, and henceforth we are in the hand of the Father.

Dr. Reid says that these seven words sweep the gamut of life. Bengel wrote that, "There are many voices making up one symphony." These sayings sing in a sevenfold chord the nature and cost of men's redemption. Surely these seven words from the cross disclose what the Savior Himself believed He was accomplishing on Calvary.

The title chosen for our coverage of these words of Jesus

is taken from a hymn composed by F. W. Faber, whose hymns and poems, even though he was an Anglican turned Roman Catholic, are second to none in sentiment and beauty.

That saintly poet, Isaac Watts, whose most expressive verses dealing with the mystery and message of the cross make him the hymnist of Calvary, was so overwhelmed by the "love so amazing, so divine," as he surveyed "the wondrous Cross, On which the Prince of Glory died," that he wrote:

> See from His head, His hands, His feet,
> Sorrow and love flow mingled down;
> Did e'er such love and sorrow meet,
> Or thorns compose so rich a crown?

God's heart, as well as Christ's, was broken at Calvary. Crucifixion itself, as endured by the Son, represented the climax of hatred heaped upon Him by His foes. But from the divine side, the cross is radiant with the love of the Trinity for a lost world, and, as we are to see, the Seven Sayings are the perfection of facets of such a sacrificial and eternal love.

> 'Tis Love! 'tis Love. Thou died'st for me!
> I hear Thy whisper in my heart!
> The morning breaks, the shadows flee;
> Pure universal Love Thou art!
> To me, to all, Thy mercies move;
> Thy Nature, and Thy Name, is Love.

The First Word of Love

LOVE THAT FORGIVES

"Father, forgive them; for they know not what they do . . ."
(*Luke 23:34*)

Love That Forgives

When he was here on earth, Jesus taught His disciples to love their enemies and to pray for those who persecuted and despitefully used them. In this first prayer on the cross, our Lord practiced what He preached, for, as Isaiah prophesied He would do, He made intercession for those who had transgressed against Him. If we truly love Jesus, who loved us even when we were His enemies, then it is essential for us to resemble Him in the willingness to forgive those who have trespassed against us. The harboring of an unforgiving spirit is alien in the heart of one confessing with the Psalmist, "I love the Lord!" Dying in such intense agony, Jesus sought divine forgiveness for us who had rejected and despised Him and nailed Him to the tree.

Two thoughts emerge from a consideration of this first utterance: the fatherly relationship and the forgiveness requested.

THE FATHERLY RELATIONSHIP

From our Lord's numerous references to the fatherhood of God there emerges a holy, unbroken intimacy between

17

God and His Son. Extended expressions such as "My Father," "Heavenly Father," "Holy Father," "Righteous Father," occur in the Gospels. But Christ's favorite form of address was the simple, single, and filial term *Father,* which first appears when He was but twelve years of age. It was then that Jesus reminded His earthly parents of the heavenly Father's prior claim to His life and service. *Father!* Who can measure the love, honor, and obedience wrapped up in such a tender noun when used by the Son of God? In His first and last saying absolute unity of spirit between Himself and God—a oneness and response to His Father's will—was maintained in spite of the terrible ordeal He faced.

With the first onslaught of pain and agony, the Savior's word, *Father,* reveals His first and instinctive thought as cruel men nailed Him to the cross, namely, His Father's identification with the cup of sacrifice He was now taking. While the repetition of the sacred term *Father,* as Jesus entered the valley of the shadow of death, declares His unshaken faith in God's will and purpose, it was also a recognition by the Son that "the suffering and injury imposed on the Father exceeded even His own agony." Does not Paul remind us that God was in Christ reconciling the world to Himself?

Dealing with the First Word of Love, Hubert Simpson fittingly observes,

> First words and last words—how revealing they are! When our Lord rose from the dead on the third day, the first word that He uttered was *Woman.* It was a prophecy of all that He and His Church were to do for the raising and blessings and hallowing of womanhood. It was Christ who emancipated womanhood and gave woman the chance to rise and rule the World. But when our Lord was nailed to the redemptive Cross, the first word that He uttered was *Father.* It tells of a trust in a loving personality that never faltered in the hour when the love and Fatherhood of God seemed to have been finally blotted out in impenetrable darkness. If ever "such pity as a father hath unto his children dear" seemed the most heartless lie in human experience it was then, when Love was being crucified with every circumstance of cruelty and outrage. If He could say *Father* then, it can always be said in confident trust.

A further truth can be gleaned from the initial word in this first saying on the cross, namely, the *ground* of the forgiveness Christ pleaded for, namely, His true Sonship. The reconciliation of sinners to God is in the Sonship of Jesus Christ. It is for His work and sake that the Father is willing to freely pardon all who repent of their sin. He knew that God is a loving Father, and naturally the Son turns to him, and Jesus' first word not only speaks of the triumph of faith in such a dark hour, but comprehends the spirit of love—a love that can draw the sting from all evil.

What must not be forgotten is that Jesus was recovering from "the swooning shock occasioned by the driving of the nails into his hands and feet," when he uttered the word *Father.* "When His fortunes were at the blackest, when He was baited by a raging pack of wolf-like enemies, and when He was sinking into unplumbed abysses of pain and desertion, He still said *Father.* It was the apotheosis of faith, and to all time it will serve as an example; because it was gloriously vindicated." For ourselves, the first word of the First Saying teaches us that our prevalence and power in God depend upon our confidence in our relationship to God. Unless sonship by faith and adoption is ours, we are destitute of the Holy Spirit who inspires the children of God to cry Abba, Father!

THE FORGIVENESS REQUESTED

In one of his prayers Jesus, addressing His Father as "Lord of heaven and earth," went on to say, ". . . neither knoweth any man the Father, save the Son" (Matt. 11:27). As the eternal Son, ever by the Father, as one brought up with Him, daily His delight, and rejoicing always before Him (Prov. 8:30), Jesus shared His Father's nature and virtues. Knowing that there was forgiveness with Him that He may be feared, Jesus revealed the compassion of His Father as One willing to abundantly pardon. And that He was in full agreement with this divine attribute is borne out in the statement that "whosoever speaketh a word against the Son of man, it shall be forgiven him" (Matt. 12:32).

Now, as Jesus dies that we might be forgiven, Jesus prays,

"Father, *forgive them.*" In this sublime sentence, Jesus not only revealed the Father's love, but His own. As Professor James Stalker expressed it, "All His life long the Father was in Him, but on the Cross the Divine life and character flamed out in His human nature like the fire in the burning bush. It uttered itself in the words, *Father, forgive them;* and what did it tell? It told that God is love." Previously, Jesus had taught His disciples to pray for those who would ill-treat them, to forgive those who trespassed against them.

Calvary's prayer for pardon is remarkable when studied in the light of the cruel treatment the Intercessor had been subjected to. From the outset of His brief ministry Jesus incurred the hatred of the Scribes and Pharisees who were bent on killing Him. And as we read those last hours before He was actually nailed to the cross, our hearts burn with indignation as one depth of baseness opens beneath another. But the magnanimous answer to all He willingly endured was *Father, forgive them!* Jesus did not urge His righteous Father to let loose judgment upon His brutal foes although they deserved it. That revenge upon those who ill-treat us is one of the sought-after satisfactions of the human heart and is certainly evidenced by some Old Testament saints "who cursed those who had persecuted and wronged them in terms of uncompromising severity." When Samson came to his tragic end, he cried out passionately in blind anger as he brought down the temple of his enemies upon them and himself, "O Lord, God, remember me, I pray thee, and strengthen me, I pray thee, only this once, O God, that I may be at once avenged of the Philistines of my two eyes."

In the divine nature there is a fire of wrath against sin, and we would not have found fault with Jesus had He called upon His Father to smite those responsible for His bitter death. But in love He prayed for the forgiveness of those who crucified Him.

Further, more than one writer has drawn attention to the fact that in His last hours Jesus did not pray, "Forgive *me.*" We have the witness of eminent, dying saints who, with the light of eternity falling upon their souls, felt an infinite distance between themselves and the perfect purity of God in whose presence they were about to enter, and died praying, "O God, forgive me, for I am unworthy to come before thee!" Jesus, however, as the sinless Son of God, had no need of penitence as He died, no sin to confess. In the final hours of His life there was no cry for God's pardon. His plea was for others: Forgive them. While among men Jesus declared that He had the authority to forgive sins, on the cross He did not exercise His divine prerogative, seeing He was the Sin-Bearer, the Substitute. Lifted up to die, Jesus calls upon God, for His sake, to forgive His crucifiers.

In Gethsemane, Jesus had qualified his prayer when he said, "Father, if it be possible, let this cup pass from me!" But on the cross He did not pray, "Father, if it be possible, forgive them." There was no doubt but that God's pardon was possible because He knew that the heart of His Father was one of pardoning grace and mercy. It is also most profitable to observe that this First Saying on the cross is introduced by an imperfect tense, "Then Jesus kept on saying, Father forgive them." The sentence has the force of such repetition. As Peter Green in his *Watchers by the Cross* puts it,

> Each blow of the hammer sent a thrill of agony through the whole of the Lord's body. And He met each fresh thrill or blow with the often-repeated prayer: "Father, forgive them, for they know not what they do." For the Greek makes it plain that this word was not spoken once. The text should be translated, "Jesus kept on saying, 'Father, forgive them, for they know not what they do.'"

Is it not comforting to know that the first word after *Father* was *forgive?* United together in our Lord's supplication is the name of God and the murderers of His Son with the connecting word *forgive* uttered by Him who came as the sole mediator between God and man. Hope thus beams from Calvary for a sinful world. Krummacher in his *Meditations on the Last Days of Christ* assures us that the words "Forgive them" reveal to us, "not merely the leaven of loving-kindness which He carries in His bosom, but it also darts like a flash of lightning through the entire night of suffering, and deciphers the mysterious position which the

Holy One of Israel here occupies as Mediator and High Priest."

They know not what they do. The ground of the pardon asked was the loving, forgiving heart of the Father, but the limitation by which such a pardon was conditioned is in the phrase, "They know not what they do," which defines its bounds. By such a clause, the Savior selects from the multitude surrounding Him those to whom the majority of them that crucified Him probably belonged. But who, exactly, were included in the *they* who were ignorant of the enormity of their sin? Without doubt, our Lord had in mind those who were primarily responsible for the crucifixion. Shortly after Jesus' death, resurrection, and ascension we find Peter saying, "If they had known, they would not have crucified the Lord of glory." "I wot that through ignorance ye did it, as did also your rulers" (1 Cor. 2:8; Acts 3:17).

Is it not hard for us to accept that those who deliberately killed the Prince of life when the choice was between Him and Barabas, the murderer, did not know what they were doing? Why, even as His crucifiers gazed upon His body spiked pitilessly to a hideous cross, they reviled Him and watched Him die a terrible death in callous indifference. Chiding Him they called upon Him to save Himself if He was the Messiah.

According to the narrative, then, those for whom Jesus prayed did not deserve His prayer, but, on the contrary, merited a curse because of their brutal treatment of Him. Who did He plead for as the nails were being driven into His hands and feet? Well, there was Peter who denied Him; Judas, who heartlessly betrayed Him; the Scribes and Pharisees, who hated Him and often plotted His death, and ultimately engineered His crucifixion. There were the Apostles who forsook Him; the false witnesses who testified against Him; the mob who railed on Him; imperious Herod and weak, vacillating Pilate; the soldiers. The marvel of marvels was that Jesus covered the guilty heads of His enemies and murderers with the shield of His love and prayed that the storm of the well-deserved wrath of a just and holy God might not break upon their heads.

In effect Jesus' prayer for His foes implies, "Do not impute to them the murderous crime they have committed upon me. Plunge their whole sinful life into the depths of the sea, and remember no more their transgressions, but consider these sinners henceforth as dead in thy sight, and act toward them as such!"

But, as Jesus died "for us men and for our salvation," His prayer for forgiveness was for us too. Of this First Word it has been said, "This word has two arms; with one it embraces all the past, with the other all the future." All sinners from the cross down to the last call of the Holy Spirit for them to repent of their sin are embraced in this prayer. Dr. James Stalker asks, "Was this prayer answered? Were the crucifiers of Jesus forgiven?" The renowned theologian then gives the answer: "To this it may be replied that a prayer for forgiveness cannot be answered without the cooperation of those prayed for. Unless they repent and seek pardon for themselves, how can God forgive them? The prayer of Jesus, therefore, meant that time should be granted them for repentance, and that they should be plied with providences and with preaching to awaken their consciences." After Calvary, there came Pentecost, when thousands repented and believed, and as the result of the Spirit's coming, multitudes were gathered in as the record in Acts declares. The unnumbered host of the redeemed in heaven will witness to an abundant answer to Calvary's prayer for forgiveness.

What must not be forgotten is the truth Scripture makes plain, namely, that we can have no part or lot in the cross unless we come to it as penitent sinners, conscious of our guilt. Any man who has no sense of sin has not taken the first step to the foot of the cross. Only the man who is prepared to own his share in the guilt of the cross may claim its share in its grace. Jesus died as the Savior of sinners, and we can have no portion with Him unless we realize our sinnership. Although Peter stated that it was through ignorance that men crucified Christ, such ignorance does not mean "innocence." It is true that Paul wrote of his life before he met Christ, "God had mercy on me, because I did it ignorantly in unbelief," but once saved by grace the

Apostle was ever conscious that he was "the chief of sinners."

Certainly, God knows about our blindness and ignorance and makes allowances and herein is our own hope and the measure of our responsibility. But ignorance does not absolve us from guilt. Of course, ignorance may lessen the guilt of sin. It may be argued that in all sin there is an element of sin. The charter of Universalism granting the assurance that all sin will be remitted and every sinner forgiven is contrary to explicit Scriptures, such as John 3:16. If a person transgresses a law of the state and is brought into court, he does not plead innocence for ignorance. As the first word in the last clause of Christ's prayer is *for*, which is substantially the same as *if*, then, we can paragraph the clause thus, "If, and so far as, they know not what they do, forgive them."

Ignorance does not obliterate the guilt of sin, and, as an old writer put it, "Ignorance does not *deserve*, but often *finds* pardon." Hubert Simpson says of the phrase "For they know not what they do," that it implies "an awful thought, namely, that sin is so terrible in its incidence and its consequences that none can ever know the extent or the measure of the harm they do." This is the thought we must read in Peter's word, "If they had known, they would not have crucified the Lord of Glory." If we walk in the light, as He is in the light, preservation from any form of ignorance in the spiritual realm will be ours.

There is much more to be learned from this First Word of Love on the cross for our comfort in cross-bearing. If "the whole world is one vast Golgotha today of crucified humanity, suffering from the deeds of men who knew not what they did," we ourselves can be made perfect through suffering. In His final agony, the first word of Jesus was a Spirit-inspired prayer, reminding us that we must not cease to pray when called upon to suffer but emulate the example of the Master who, by prayer, preserved the serenity of His soul, and who now by His intercession in heaven, inspires His fellow-sufferers in their dark hour. Calvary teaches us that "Love suffers long, and is kind . . . beareth all things."

The Second Word of Love

LOVE THAT TRANSFORMS

*"Verily I say unto thee, Today shalt thou be with me
in paradise"
(Luke 23:34)*

Love That
Transforms

The sayings of the dying are always impressive, as I
sought to prove in my book, *Last Words of Saints and
Sinners*. But above the final sayings of famous men, the
dying utterances of Jesus will be treasured forever, seeing
they are charged with eternal significance. Professor William
Clow reminds us that "Words are always photographs, more
or less true, of the mind that utters them; these, our Lord
uttered, were the truest words ever spoken, because He
stamped upon them the image of Himself." In response to
the cry of the dying thief, "Lord, remember me," the crucified Savior answered in precious words that have dried the
tears of millions of mourners and lifted the cold shadow of
death from countless myriads down the ages.

We have entitled this Second Word of Love, *Love That
Transforms*, for the remarkable change in the malefactor
who believed. Human life provides us with many illustra-
tions of the way the fervent love of one can transform the
character of another. William Booth shared his Savior's love

for the drunks and prostitutes of London's dark corners and
had the joy of seeing many of them wonderfully changed and
fashioned into early leaders of his Salvation Army. Like
Michelangelo, the old general saw the angel in a slab of
stone and lovingly released it. It was so with Christ and the
thief who came to experience the truth enshrined in the
lines of E. M. Grimes:

> Break through my nature, mighty heavenly Love,
>   Clear every avenue of thought and brain,
> Flood my affections, purify my will,
>   Let nothing but Thine own pure life remain.

In this Second Word of Love there are two general
thoughts to explore: the malefactor's plea, "Lord, remember
me" and the Master's promise, "Today thou shalt be with
me in paradise."

Before we concentrate on this Second Word itself, a survey
of the three crosses as a whole might prove profitable. Surely
there has never been such a tragic spectacle in the history
of the world as witnessed that day when Jesus died between
two thieves! This somber scene has inspired painters and
poets alike. Those three crucified individuals that formed
the center of attraction were alike in this predicament in
that each of them had arrived at "the last stage of his earthly
pilgrimage and was hovering on the solemn and awful brink
of a momentous eternity." But He who hangs in the middle,
although exposed to a raging storm, takes in the sails for a
peaceful entrance into the haven of repose.

We see the other two, on the contrary, almost shipwrecked
and threatened with the most dreadful ruin, struggling with
the billows. They had opened their hearts to delusion and
were carried along unrestrainedly from sin to sin until ar-
rested as murderers. They were crucified as an atonement to
public justice. There would have been a tragic dignity in a
lonely cross standing solitary against the sky, but there were
two other crosses to which were nailed common robbers, as
if to emphasize what Jesus' crucifiers thought of His character.

"They crucified Him, and *two others* with Him" (John 19:18). These *three!* What a remarkable triad this is! Why were there only three on that crucifixion day? And why these particular three? On that hill long and gray outside the city wall, God's arranging hand can be seen in the way the three sufferers had been placed. Man meant only to increase the shame of the sinless Christ by putting Him between two notorious criminals as if He were the worst of the three, "On either side one, and Jesus in the midst." God, however, over-ruled in the placing of the two thieves in order to represent the two great classes into which the whole of humanity is divided both now and in eternity: the saved and the lost.

It was no casual action that prompted the soldiers to hang Jesus between two thieves, for during His ministry He companied with publicans and sinners and now He dies among them. If Jesus had chosen to be the friend of sinners when He was living, let Him be found dead in the same uncongenial company. Taken together then, these three crosses afford us an image of the world, with the Man on the middle cross set for the rising of one thief and for the falling of the other—a Savior of life unto life to the one and of death unto death for the other. By crucifying Jesus between two sinners the authorities hoped to set the seal on His contemptibleness, but actually they helped Him carry out His eternal scheme of redemption.

On the center cross hung the King of Love, numbered among transgressors; and on the other two crosses were slaves of sin, dying for the sins they had committed. Because all three victims died together they depict three relative truths. In fact, the spiritual suggestions of this grim triad are numberless.

One dies *for* sin; one dies *to* sin; one dies *in* sin. The two thieves were dying for their own iniquities, but the Man on the middle cross was dying for the other two men and for all they represent. Thus we have a *dying saint,* a *dying Savior, a dying sinner.* Viewing these grim crosses we are found hanging on one of three; such a scene presents the separation Christ brings about.

THE CROSS OF REDEMPTION

We look first at the cross in the center. It is the greatest of the three in that its truth is not only the central revelation of Scripture but the central point in all history. The heart of Christianity is the Bible, and the heart of the Bible is the cross, and the heart of the cross is the very heart of God who was in Christ reconciling the world unto Himself. Crucifixion, the form of capital punishment conceived by the Romans, and abolished by Emperor Constantine, as meted out to Jesus, the sinless One, forms the darkest blot on the pages of history. At the old rugged cross we see man at his worst, but God at His best.

What infinite condescension it was on the part of the Lord to make Himself of no reputation, to be willing to be reckoned among transgressors, and to be thought of as the chief of the three dying that day! There He was in agony and shame dying *like* sinners, dying *among* sinners, but dying *for* sinners. No wonder the old divines revered the cross as "The Divine Academy of Love." At Calvary we see, at least, a fourfold accomplishment: a love manifested, a law satisfied, a liberty secured, and a life to be lived.

A LOVE MANIFESTED

What wondrous love Jesus revealed when He was willing to bleed and die.

> Inscribed upon the Cross, we see,
> In shining letters, *God is Love.*

Nature eloquently extols God's power and wisdom but is silent as to His love for sinners. It is only at Calvary that we learn Jesus loves us without stint and reserve. In the surrender of His beloved Son as the sinner's substitute, God broke His alabaster box of precious ointment: "Love so amazing, so divine, demands my soul, my life, my all."

A LAW SATISFIED

By His death, Jesus met and discharged the exacting demands of the divine law decreeing death for disobedience.

"The soul that sinneth it shall die." Along with such a condemnation was a curse, "Cursed is every one who continueth not in the book of the Law." But Jesus took our condemnation and curse and made them His own. He bore our curse and carried out the penalty so that we could sing, "Free from the law, O happy condition, Jesus has bled, and there is remission."

That middle cross is the charter of our pardon, the guarantee of our acceptance with God and heirship. Delivered from the guilt, penalty, and reign of sin, we are enthralled in glad bondage to our Redeemer.

A LIBERTY SECURED

While it may appear somewhat repugnant to refined yet Christless minds to sing about being "Washed in the blood of the Lamb," it is ever true that there is power in the blood the Savior shed for sinners. John was not ashamed to join in the Calvary doxology, and sing, "Unto him that loveth us, and loosed us from our sins in his blood" (Rev. 1:5, RV).

Although we cannot understand the miracle of it, we believe the fact that the blood of Jesus is able to make a heart whiter than the snow. And we have seen too many sin-bound captives gloriously emancipated to doubt the ever-continuing efficacy of Christ's finished work. Ours is the solemn obligation to "stand fast in the liberty wherewith Christ hath made us free" (Gal. 5:1).

A LIFE TO BE LIVED

It is one thing to believe in a crucified Christ and a different matter altogether to live a crucified life, yet the latter should be the fruit of the former. The provision of the cross not only cancels out our past but covers our present. Christ died that we might live—live in the fullest and highest sense. This was the truth Paul emphasized when he declared that the crucified, risen, and exalted Christ lived in him (Gal. 2:20). As we know, Paul's Epistles are drenched with the message and mission of the cross, for he was one who "determined to know nothing among men save Christ, and

Him crucified." In one verse, Paul gives us a marvelous triad to summarize his teaching on the cross for which he suffered much persecution. This triad is found in his Galatian epistle, every chapter of which gives us a different glimpse of Calvary. As there were *three* crosses outside the city wall, so Paul wrote of three crosses. "God forbid that I should glory, save in the cross of our Lord Jesus Christ, by whom the world is crucified unto me, and I unto the world" (Gal. 6:14). Here we have *Christ on a cross, the world on a cross, the believer on a cross.*

The first cross was that of our Lord, and what dreary desolation it was for Him, yet it meant life and peace for us.

The second cross holds the present world which was dead insofar as Paul was concerned. The world, to the Apostle, was a "hollow thing, a lie, a vanity, tinsel and paint." The world's idols had fallen from their high estate, and other motives, grander and more beneficial, governed his life. Can we say that the world is crucified—dead, having no appeal?

The third cross brings us to a realization of the mystic truth about being crucified with Christ, imitating His sacrifice, sharing His death. Paul could write to the Philippians about being made conformable to Christ's death. Is ours the crucified life? Are we dead to the appeal of the world of which Satan is its god? Do we know what it is to be raised again and to have left all the sins that once held us in their thrall in the grave of Christ? "Dying with Jesus, by death reckon'd mine; living with Jesus a new life divine."

THE CROSS OF RECEPTION

This was a cross of the thief whose spiritual biography was brief but blessed. In the morning he was in *Nature,* lost and condemned; at midday, he was in *Grace,* his black past erased; by midnight he was in *Glory,* sharing its bliss with the One who had redeemed him. That dying thief was the first trophy of Christ's redemptive work. Had He not declared, "I, if I be lifted up, will draw all men unto me"? Well, here was the first fulfillment of that prophecy. Here we find Christ illustrating His threefold office of Prophet, Priest, and King.

As the Prophet, Christ said to the daughters of Jerusalem, "Weep not for me, but for yourselves, and for the days that are coming."

As the Priest, He prayed, "Father, forgive them," and cried in triumph, "It is finished."

As the King, He opened the door of heaven for a believing soul to enter. "Today shalt thou be with me."

What a manifestation of the omnipotence of saving grace we have in this repentant thief exchanging his deep-dying scarlet for a robe of righteousness whiter than snow! Here we have a Savior "able to save to the uttermost," and He bids us despair of none. Only one of the two thieves was saved that none might despair, but *only* one that none might presume.

There are, at least, two truths emerging from a consideration of this Cross of Reception which perhaps was on the right of the middle cross, seeing that the right hand of the Lord brings salvation.

The triumph of faith. The evangel says, "He that believeth and is baptized shall be saved." But all the dying thief could do was to believe, and a naked faith in Christ's promise saved him. Had he lived, he would undoubtedly have confessed his Lord in the waters of baptism. Sinners are saved by grace, through *faith*. Further, when Jesus said, "Today thou shalt be with me," He implied that there would be no unconsciousness period between death and glory, as some would have us believe. The thief did not have to pass through purgatorial fires before he could enter paradise. He departed with Christ.

The triumph of grace. This thief was saved at the eleventh hour. Certainly we believe in deathbed conversions—that whenever and wherever a sinner repents and turns to the Savior an immediate salvation is experienced. "Whosoever cometh to me I will in no wise cast out." But it is suicidal to put the matter of our soul's eternal welfare off to our deathbed. We may never have one. Ours may be a sudden death. Further, if bedridden, we may come to our last days bereft of reason, unconscious, and utterly unable to hear an appeal and respond. Some of my saddest moments have been those when, standing by the bedside of the dying, I knew that they were not able to hear and appreciate my words.

Then, is it not somewhat mean and contemptible to give the best of our lives to the devil and at the last offer Jesus the rag-tag of a wasted life? Yet there is no limit to His mercy, although the dying thief and murderer just had time to cry, "Lord, remember me," grace prevailed and the blood Jesus was shedding made the vilest clean.

THE CROSS OF REJECTION

Standing beneath this dark, tragic cross we learn that *the only impediment* to salvation and eternal peace is a hard, impenitent heart, for this second thief died as he lived, in his callousness and sin. This unrepentant, unsaved criminal was as near to Christ as his now repentant companion in crime and could have received the same assurance of pardon as he did, but there was no cry for mercy. Even at such a last moment the Savior would have saved him if he had chosen to seek the Lord, but he remained blaspheming to the end. Jesus *can* save the unholy, the unfit, and the unclean, but the unwilling He cannot save. In His compassion, He never asks any man about the extent of his sin, but only about the reality of his desire to be freed from iniquity forever.

Thus, from one side a thief goes to paradise, and from the other side, the companion thief goes to perdition. Here we have the universal law enacted that Christ is either the savior of life, or of death. On that low, lone hill of Calvary, we have a picture of how the cross of Christ divides the world. Wherever He is still lifted up in testimony and offer, there are those who repent and believe on one side and the scornful and unbelieving on the other. The preaching of the cross is either the power of God unto salvation, or foolishness. We do not know. Perhaps those two thieves were natural brothers, brought up in the same good home, yet passed out into a life of sin together and ultimately made to suffer death together for their crimes. The difference is that one received the Savior, but the other rejected Him.

This sad and somber cross of the unrepentant thief emphasizes two inescapable thoughts:

He wanted a Christ without the cross. Both of the thieves cried, "If thou be the Christ save thyself and us." The one who believed came to discover that Christ could save him from sin, although Christ did not deliver him from the penalty of his sin. It was he who confessed of the dying Savior, "This man hath done nothing amiss"; and received Him as the sinner's substitute. But the other thief clung to his desire of a bloodless gospel: If the bleeding Savior is the miracle-working One, then let Him come down from His cross and save us.

The modern cry is for a Christ without a blood-stained cross, and so we hear a great deal about the ethical Christ, the social Christ, Christ the teacher. But Christ and His cross are eternally nailed together. Paul could say, "We preach Christ crucified," and this is the only preaching the Spirit blesses and can use for the conviction of the sinner's conscience as to the loathsomeness of his sin and deliverance from it. The preaching of the cross is ever the power of God unto salvation.

He died with his sin's remedy at hand. It was impossible for Christ to be any nearer to either of the thieves than He was. Truly, He was at hand to bless, and one of them received His benediction. The other criminal was as close to the Savior but failed to take his opportunity of accepting the proffered mercy. There may be some excuse for those who have never heard of God's redeeming grace and power and who have no law by which they cannot realize their lost and hopeless condition; but those who live in a land of Bibles, churches, and Christian influences are without excuse. In so many ways they are constantly reminded of their perilous state without Christ and are often exhorted to forsake their sin. But they prefer to stay on their Cross of Rejection, and so, many of them die in their sin. There is no sin so disastrous as callous rejection, and there is no end so dark and hopeless as that of one who deliberately refuses Jesus as the only Savior.

Many years ago in the now defunct *Sunday School Times,*

W. Everett Henry had a most impressive poem summarizing the truths suggested by *The Three Crosses:*

The Cross of Impenitence

The wood was hard and held the nails;
The soft flesh gave with aching pain.
Dread mockery beat down the wails
Of stricken friends; there came again
In dripping bitterness a voice,
"If thou be Christ, then save us three
From death." His hardened heart made choice
Of darkening death's black certainty;
His twisted soul could not relent;
He knew no word that spelled "repent."

The Cross of Penitence

The wood was hard and held the nails;
The soft flesh gave with aching pain.
Some tears dropped down, and gales
Of ribald mirth could not restrain
The plea, "Remember me, Thou King
To Be." And hard against the clash
Of darkest sins, with sovereign ring
Came words of gentleness to smash
Sin's shackles off the soul: "Thou'lt be
Today in Paradise with me."

The Cross of Mercy

The wood was hard and held the nails;
The soft flesh gave with aching pain.
A shameful shame the Son assails,
And sin's black waves roll on amain;
But majesty rests on Christ's brow,
Compassion dwells in his distress;
Omnipotence rides in the now
A humble penitent to bless.
The Lord of mercy, flaming Light,
Endows the cross with ageless might.

THE MALEFACTOR'S PLEA

It was St. Fulgentius who called the Second Word, *The Testament of Christ written with the pen of the Cross.* And it is fitting that the record of this Word is only to be found in Luke's Gospel, which is the Gospel of the beauty of the Redeemer's life. While it is "the Gospel of the Holy angels; the Gospel of ecstatic song and liturgic chant, heavenly and earthly," it is also a Pauline-like Gospel of triumphant grace and of abounding forgiveness. Luke is the Gospel of the *lost,* seeing it contains the Savior's mission of intent: "For the Son of man is come to seek and to save that which was lost" (Luke 19:10). Luke also gives the account of his reception by, and of lost sinners (15:1, 2) and the story of the Prodigal Son (15:21–32) which parable is "an epitome of the whole teaching of Christ, as the salvation of the thief on the cross is the life of Christ in miniature." The story of the Prodigal Son and the incident of the dying, penitent thief are identical in that they reveal the nature of sin and of forgiveness.

Then it is Luke who gives us the account of a lost sinner like Zacchaeus (19:1–10) and who likewise paints for us the exquisite picture of a woman's passionate penitence (7:36–50) in contrast to the most complete picture of man's sterner and more restrained penitence (23:41, 42).

Scripture gives us only two or three verses to describe the biography of the malefactor transformed by the sacrificial love he saw manifested in the One next to him dying a similar death.

His sinful career. With his companion he is called a "thief," not only by Luke, but by Matthew (27:44) and Mark (15:32). Dr. William Clow points out that "when a man is called a thief, the name suggests a very common and degraded sinner; but it is pointed out that *robber* would be the correct name, and that probably he and his companion may have been revolutionaries, whose opposition to the Roman rule had driven them outside the pale of society where, to win a subsistence, they had to resort to the trade of highwaymen; but in that country, tyrannized over by a despotic foreign power, those who attempted to raise the standard of revolt were sometimes far more ignoble characters, though the necessities of their position betrayed them into acts of violence."

Both Luke (23:32, 33) and John (18:30) use the term *malefactor* which implies an evil-doer or a criminal. And when the penitent thief confessed, "We receive the due rewards of our *deeds,*" such language suggests that both thieves had memories stained with acts for which they considered death to be the lawful penalty. The sacred record makes it clear that at first both thieves reviled the dying Jesus. They joined in the mockery of the chief priests: "He saved others; himself he cannot save. . . . The thieves also . . . cast the same in his teeth" (Matt. 27:41–44). Mark has it, "They that were crucified with him reviled him" (15:32). Perhaps we think it strange that they would curse a fellow-sufferer, but we can see in their past life the reason. The two thieves may have been members of a bandit gang who combined revolutionary aims with their banditry. Striving to overturn the established order by force they likewise attacked things settled and ancient and thought of Jesus as "a mere coward who had feared to strike a blow against a system which He denounced."

It would seem that these two national insurgents were both strong in evil, as such companions in crime commonly are, but one appears to be harder and bolder than the other: The *evil genius* who felt that a Messiah of earth was the only one he was willing to fight and die for. On the other hand the thief who became the first answer to Christ's first prayer for divine forgiveness was evidently more susceptible to spiritual influences than his associate in crime. Knowing something of the gentle Galilean's ministry of love and of His dignity during the drama of His trial and serenity on the cross, the malefactor revealed himself as one cast in a softer mold than the other sinner. Those first words of Jesus, as the nails were being driven through his hands and feet, "Father, forgive them," struck his heart like a dart and constrained him to turn to the Savior in penitence and faith.

His startling confession. Because "repentance ripens quickly in the soil of the Cross," the thief, made conscious of his need as a sinner, stands out as a striking illustration of instantaneous conversion. The utterance from his dying lips is impressive.

1. He confessed his sin and that of his companion, "We indeed justly; for we receive the due reward of our deeds."

2. He declared his own act of faith in his prayer, "Jesus! remember me when thou comest into thy kingdom."

3. He manifested the truest concern for his sinful friend, "Dost thou not fear God, seeing thou art in the same condemnation?"

It is beyond us to explain how it was that this dying thief gained an insight into divine things and a grasp of real values in the spiritual realm in such a short time. Expressing his fear of falling into the hands of a living God, he reached his last hours with no false notions of personal guilt or of the justice of punishment he deserved. Confessing the sinlessness of Jesus, he was fully aware of his own sinfulness and sought the divine forgiveness the Man next to Him had prayed for and became the last disciple Jesus was to win before He died.

The crucified thief, who was our Lord's last companion before He died, was the first trophy of the efficaciousness of His blood and the first sinner to enter heaven washed in the blood of the Lamb. Truly grace abounded that dark day when an outcast felon, a man with a tainted past and a tarnished name, became a new creature in Christ Jesus and a perpetual witness to His power to save even the worst of sinners, as well as a constant encouragement to them to repent. The centurion who had superintended the crucifixion was another convert who, unashamedly, confessed the deity of Jesus.

His sudden conversion. What a marvelous day, the last day of the dying thief was! Think of it, he was,

> In the morning in a state of *Guilt,*
> At noon in a state of *Grace,*
> During the night in a state of *Glory!*

We do not minimize the wonder of this bad man's change of heart because it took place instantaneously as he reached the verge of eternity. Although a cruel cross was his deathbed, he manifested repentance toward God and faith in Jesus

Christ, and his salvation was immediate, joyful and complete. A writer of centuries ago said with justice: "On the cross, the nails had fastened the hands and feet. In that supreme suffering nothing remained free. Yes! something: heart and tongue. By the gracious inspiration of God the dying thief presented to God all in him that was free, so that with the heart he believed unto righteousness, and with the mouth made confession unto salvation."

The penitent thief was saved then, "while his heart was beating out the last minutes of the day of grace for him." Scientific investigators may tell us that all our processes of mental life are continuous and that nothing happens which is not prepared for by previous conditions and that what looks like a sudden conversion is really the climax of a long series of events, but there is no evidence that this thief had previous religious conditions which resulted in his deathbed repentance. There can be absolutely no question about God's ability to save in a moment of time, for I experienced it myself almost seventy years ago.

Had salvation been by good works, the thief would never have been saved, or if baptism had been essential, his cross would have been the tree of doom. He had no church, no Bible—only a n.ked faith in the Savior's grace. Many a pastor can tell of those who, with no previous religious interest or connection, were won for Christ before their end came. To deny the possibility, the reality of such a sudden change, is to deny that whoever calls upon God for salvation at any given moment cannot be saved to the uttermost.

One of the tragedies of Calvary is that only one of the two thieves repented and turned to the Savior. One only was saved that none might despair, but only one that none might presume. On the middle cross there were two gaunt arms stretched out to save, but only one arm embraces a sinner conscious of his need of a Savior. There would have been the same salvation and glorious future for the unrepentant thief, but he died in rejection and was left to his terrible fate. This hardened child of unbelief was urged by his companion in crime to acknowledge his sin and fear God, but because God's mercy is never arbitrarily bestowed, the impenitent scoffer went out into the blackness of darkness forever.

THE MASTER'S PROMISE

Surely there is no episode comparable to what happened at Calvary when a penitent thief received such a kingly response from the Man of Sorrows. The humble prayer of faith he offered must have gratified Jesus and brought Him a foretaste of satisfaction for His travail of soul. Coarse, foul lips, now purged, were the last to utter a good word for the innocent One dying such an ignominious death. As it has been expressed, "The story is like a flower of beauty amongst those dreary crags of agony." What amazes us is the fact that the miracle of transformation was accomplished *before* Jesus spoke to the thief. Dr. William Clow says that it was not by words that Jesus converted the malefactor:

> Jesus did not address the penitent thief at all till the thief spoke to Him. The work of conviction was done before He uttered a word. Yet it was His work; and how did He do it? Peter exhorted Godly wives to win their husbands for the Saviour by their "behaviour," which the term "conversation" implies. It was by the impression of His patience, His innocence, His peace, and His magnanimity, that Jesus converted the man; and herein He has left us an example that we should follow in His steps. But His words, when He did speak, although they were few added immensely to the impression.

The cause of the promise. The concise, comforting message found in the Second Word of Love was occasioned by the previous utterances of the thief who, as he looked at the dying form of Jesus, from his smitten heart confessed two wonders:

> The wonders of His glorious love,
> And my own worthlessness.

Doubtless Jesus had heard this thief, who was to pass through the serried ranks of angels and company with Him in paradise, rebuke his fellow bandit by saying, "If thou be Christ, save thyself and us." The rebuke he received must

have consoled the heart of Jesus as He entered the agony of
the cross: "Dost not thou fear God, seeing thou art in the
same condemnation? And we indeed justly; for we receive
the due reward of our deeds, but this man hath done nothing
amiss."

Then the thief turned and spoke to Jesus: "Lord, remember me when thou comest into thy kingdom." Both thieves
must have heard that First Word—the amazing prayer for
forgiveness, not for Himself, but for others—and the one
who believed was deeply moved by the grace of the Savior
and wished not to be forgotten. The Revised Version has a
beautiful touch. "I see your name is Jesus. Remember me,
Jesus, when you come into your kingdom." The thief had
heard humanity's great High Priest interceding for sinners
and quickly realized that He was dying to make atonement
for them. John Calvin was right when he wrote that he
questioned "if ever since the world began there has been so
bright an example of faith." The pregnant saying of Tholuck
asked, "Did ever the new birth take place in so strange a
cradle?"

Although the thief must have been horrible to look at,
all blood-bespattered as he hung on the cross, yet he it was
who gave the onlookers, who must have heard him speak to
Jesus, a rare glimpse into the divine glory of the Savior
whose cross was to be for him "a ladder up to heaven." He
"spoke to Jesus as to a king and prayed to Him as to a God."
Some scholars affirm that the term *Lord* in this robber's
speech is unauthentic. But if, as Krummacher suggests, the
term as used in the Authorized Version is *kyrie,* a title of
majesty, then the thief spoke to Jesus not as a rabbi or
teacher, but by his words he "brings out of the appearance of
a worm that is trodden upon, the heavenly King of Glory."

Such a conception of the Man crowned with thorns is in
keeping with the penitent sinner's desire to be remembered
by Him when He entered His kingdom. Over His cross was
the title "The King of the Jews," and in His reply to the
criminal's appeal to appear with Jesus in His regal glory, He
stated: "I am a King already. I will take thee with me into
paradise. With this bleeding hand will I open to thee the

gates of the world of blessedness." As we proceed in our meditation of Seven Words of Love, we shall describe how each element of shame in the cross is turned by the divine alchemy into a thing of glory.

How simple, brief, and yet expressive was the plea of the penitent, "Lord, remember me." No demanding ambition as the woman had who told the Lord to seat her two sons, one on the right, and the other on the left in His kingdom. A swift understanding of the person of his august companion was granted the thief who prayed. The thief called Him, "this *Man* has done nothing amiss," and the gentleness, innocence, and dignity of Christ broke his heart. It was then he avowed the kingship of Jesus as he witnessed His calm, serene, and kingly attitude. The transformed robber hoped that when Jesus came as the king of Israel at some far-off date that He would remember His humble companion in the dishonor of the punishment of Calvary. But as we shall see, he got far more than he requested or dreamed of.

The wonder of it all is that Jesus accepted the homage of the petitioner as he testified to His humanity, innocence, and kingship. As William Clow puts it, "This great sinner laid on Christ the weight of his soul, the weight of his sins, the weight of his eternity; and Christ accepted the burden."

The certainty of the promise. How magnificent and magnanimous was the answer of Jesus to the penitent who had only asked to be remembered by Him in the great day of His kingdom! The Savior promised him the closest of companionship before the day was out. Little did the penitent dream that in a few hours he would be our Lord's first companion at the gate of paradise. What amazing grace! Jesus accomplished for the thief "exceeding abundantly above all" he had asked. The certainty of the fulfillment of His promise made to the saved thief is apparent in the first five words of this Second Word, "Verily I say unto you." Such an authoritative statement anticipated the resurrection fiat, "All power is given unto me in heaven and in earth." Although Jesus was dying in all His weakness and loneliness, yet He claims all power. He had called Himself "the Truth," and as such He had authority to fulfill all He promised.

"Verily!" This word of surety which Jesus used more than seventy times is equivalent to one of His names: Amen (Rev. 3:14). "Amen, I say unto thee" was an absolute, unhesitating self-assertion characteristic of Jesus' teaching. Dr. William Alexander in his *Verbum Crucis* cites the gathered sentence:

> This at once enables us to perceive the meaning of the *Amen* so often used in the Gospels. The double *Amen* occurs as the prelude to sentences of Christ 25 times in John's Gospel alone. The single *Amen* occurs about 30 times in Matthew. It is half assertive, half liturgical. To those simple men as they rocked with Him in the boat, in the long golden hush of the summer evenings by the Lake of Galilee, came His *Amen*. It was like the hymn of their nursery, and the chant of their synagogue. It was also the expression of *certainty*. It told the resolution of their simple doubts; of a fixed heaven over the fleeting waters of human opinion.

As used by Jesus on the cross, "verily" implied absolute certainty of realization. His great utterance was not introduced by "I think," "I hope," "I infer," but "Amen, I say," and in such an utterance we make an act of faith because we believe Him to be the Truth. "Verily I say." Jesus' own will was the reason for transforming the thief into a companion in paradise. "I say." These inspired words imply He has the sole right to speak and that He will have mercy on whom He will have mercy. Was He not dying as a King? And as such His word was with power. His crucifiers looked upon Him as another felon dying on a wooden gibbet, but Jesus asserted His majestic authority as He turned to a newly secured convert and gave him the plainest assurance of paradise. As for the thief, he had the absolutely indisputable confidence that though he must die, he would live forever in the company of his Savior.

The content of the promise. At eventide there shall be light, and from the darkness of the cross there streamed light to enlighten the eyes of the dying thief and to guide him into glory. "Today shalt thou be with me in paradise." Turning again to that central Figure on that hill we see Jesus assuming different roles. He is before us as the prophesied Substitute, numbered with transgressors, bearing the iniquity of all. As the unceasing Intercessor, Jesus pleads for sinners to be pardoned. As the great High Priest, He grants full absolution to the dying thief whose message to him has been called, "The first High Priestly words of absolution from the Cross." As the mighty King, He bestowed gifts a thousandfold greater than the suppliant dreamed of. Krummacher finds in the contact between the Redeemer and the robber an actual exposition of the Savior's declaration, "I am the way, the truth, and the life."

> *Way:* Who is it that serves the malefactor on His right, in opposition to His fellow-sufferer on the left, as a bridge on which he may pass from a state of curse to that of grace?
> *Truth:* Who is it that enlightens him by that marvellous light whose rays penetrate into his inmost soul, and expel all the phantoms of delusion from him?
> *Life:* Who is it that takes from his bosom the consciousness of a state of death, and replaces it with the most blissful and vital hope?—yea, that imparts to his soul, even on this side of eternity, a new life of peace, supernatural joy, during consciousness of adoption, and the most heartfelt longing after Heaven. Is it not the crucified Saviour Who is the Author of it all?

The content of the promise Jesus gave to the thief represents the boundless power and wonderful efficacy of His merits, as the One who died for our sins according to the Scriptures. When Jesus said, "Today [or this day] shalt thou be with me in paradise," He offered stupendous proof that His vicarious death sufficed for the sinner's justification and glorification. Bossuet, the renowned European theologian gave us the threefold outline: (1) *Today*—what promptitude; (2) *with me*—what company; (3) *in paradise*—what repose.

Today. The thief only asked for recollection in the dim future of distant ages, but the faint hope in his dying heart was not for some far-off day. At the end of that terrible day, with all its anguish, he would be lost in the surging crowds of the redeemed. Once he drew his last breath he would be launched out of time into eternity. *Today* is an expression that can mean "within measurable distance," and for the dying malefactor it could only have been some three or four hours after receiving the royal promise that he surrendered the cross for a crown, and as a forgiven beggar, he was lifted from the dunghill and placed among princes. In his plea, he said, *"When* thou comest into thy kingdom." Jesus responded by saying, *Today* shall be the blissful moment of your entrance into paradise. In a moment of time this prodigal arose and went to be with the Father he had just heard Jesus pray to.

With me. It would appear that Jesus died just a short while before the robber and that He was on the other side of death waiting to receive him. Says Dr. Clow, "All Heaven is in these two words, with Me. What do we really know of Heaven, what do we wish to know, except that it is to be *with Christ?"* How wonderful it is to realize that this convert of only a few minutes had his hard heart softened, all his guilt pardoned, and his soul saved and safe forever. The highest privilege the King had promised to His most faithful servants is accorded to the thief, "Where I am, there ye may be also" (John 12:36; 14:3). Paul shared the same promise Jesus gave the thief when he wrote that after death he would be "with Christ, which is far better." In his plea, the thief said, "Lord, *remember me."* Jesus replied, "Today shalt thou be *with me."* For the joy set before him of sitting down with his Savior in paradise, like his Lord, the thief was strengthened to endure his cross.

In paradise. If the language of Jesus means anything, it is surely that there is no such sphere as "purgatory." The thief, saved by grace at the eleventh hour, had no time to prepare for sainthood, and at death he did not pass through purgatorial fires to be fit to abide in the presence of his Lord. Immediately he died, he was with Christ. As C. H. Spurgeon expressed it, "You shall not lie in purgatory for ages, nor sleep in limbo for so many years; but you shall be ready for bliss at once, and at once you shall enjoy it. The sinner was hard by the gates of Hell, but almighty mercy lifted him up and the Lord said, *'Today* shalt thou be with me in paradise.' "

As the thief's transformation was instantaneous from that of a loathsome sinner into a disciple of the Lord, so, through grace, his translation from death into life forevermore with Christ was just as instant. As soon as he believed, he received the seal of his faith in the assurance that he would go immediately to be with the One who had saved him. The moment he was absent from the Lord, he would be at home with Him in another world.

Further, the comforting promise of Christ implies the continuity of life after death claims the body. Did Jesus not proclaim Himself to be "the Life," and after His death on the cross was He not alive forevermore? The dying thief, then, could not share the presence of the Eternal One without sharing the eternal life to be found in Him. Life does not cease the moment a person expires. Death is only associated with the body. Whether life after death continues in heaven or hell depends upon one's relationship to Jesus Christ, who suffered death that they might share His risen, glorified life.

But what are we to understand by the "paradise" Jesus promised the penitent robber? In biblical Hebrew the word is used to describe a choice garden and is thus applied to the abode of Adam and Eve in Eden. The idea of a lovely garden would not "call up in the consciousness of the dying man a scene of beauty, innocence and peace, where, washed clean from the defilement of his past sins, he would begin to exist again as a new creature."

Paul wrote of being "caught up even to the third heaven caught up into paradise," which means he was given a revelation of the present condition of departed saints. Rest and refreshment are implied by the word "paradise." In his conversation with the thief Jesus used "paradise" for the only time. Usually, in His teaching of the blissful, eternal abode He referred to it as "heaven" or his "Father's house." It has been suggested that the penitent thief, suffering from thirst, agony, and shame, needed the consolation symbolized by the popular conception of paradise consisting of, as Josephus expresses it, "Habitations beyond the ocean, in a region that is neither oppressed with storms of rain, or snow, or with intense heat, but that this place is such as is refreshed by the gentle breathing of a west wind, that is perpetually blowing from the ocean." And from the Septuagint we gather this description, "For unto you is Paradise opened, the tree of life is planted, the time to come is prepared, plenteousness is made ready, a city is builded and rest is allowed; yea, perfect goodness and wisdom. The root of evil is sealed up from you, weakness and the moth is hid from you, and corruption is fled into Hell to be forgotten: Sorrows are passed, and in the end is showed the treasure of immortality" (2 Esdras 8:53–54).

All this, and more, would be in our Lord's mind as He spoke to the thief of "paradise," which is the transliteration of the Greek word used in the Septuagint of the Garden of Eden in its pristine peace, glory, and beauty. Genesis gives us a seven-fold description. It is the place of

1. Light: eastward—toward the sun (2:8).
2. Life: knowledge (2:9).
3. Refreshment (2:10).
4. Happy service of God (3:8).
5. Abundant food (2:16).
6. The presence of God (3:8).
7. The voice of God (3:10).

Whatever conception of paradise the dying malefactor might have had is not known. For him, he was to be the companion of Jesus in the place to which He was about to go, and that was sufficient consolation in his tortured condition.

What are some of the abiding lessons we learn as we conclude our meditation on The Second Word Of Love? The first one is that we are not to treat the immediate transformation of the dying thief as an exceptional, solitary act of Christ's redeeming power. As He is ever ready to save to the uttermost all who turn to Him in penitence and faith, such a marvel of grace exhibited on the cross has been repeated many times since then. The Savior is ever ready to make any "rebel, a priest and a king."

A further lesson is that there was only a step between the thief and death with hell beyond, and he made it a step of repentance and thus did not die in sin as his companion in crime and condemnation did. As we are all within measurable distance of heaven or hell, how essential it is to know whether we are prepared to meet our God. How tragic it is for anyone experiencing an unexpected death not to have been at peace with God beforehand! To those who have cried, "Lord, remember me," sudden death is sudden glory.

Another lesson we gather from the dramatic encounter between the robber and the Redeemer is the comfort the dying person can gather from the revelation of paradise. To know that as soon as the veil of flesh is torn away from one dying in Christ, Light Everlasting shines on them in a land where there are no tears and graves is indeed an incomparable balm for sorrowing hearts left behind. *Today—paradise.* Out of time into eternity.

Further, in a most literal sense the central cross makes every other cross bearable, and thus the penitent thief could say, "I am crucified with Christ." There is a beautiful legend to the effect that as Jesus said, "Today shalt thou be with me in paradise," the shadow of Christ's cross fell upon the cross of the repentant one, sheltering him from the burning heat of the sun—typical, surely, of the eternal shelter from the fires of hell through the death of the Savior. The moment the thief cried, *"Lord, remember me,"* the miracle happened, the crisis of conversion was over. Those who deliberately sin against God and quench the Spirit, trusting to a death-bed repentance to settle the score with heaven, often are cast suddenly into the blackness of darkness forever.

Krummacher reminds us that the criminal who was converted in a moment of time and shortly after passed through the gates of paradise amid the acclamation of angels was "the first herald who by his appearing there brought the glorified spirits the intelligence that Christ had won the great battle of our deliverance. As the first fruits of the sufferings of the Divine Surety, as well as of the blessed human harvest which should spring up from the wondrous seed of His blood." The glory of redeeming grace is its power to conquer the stubbornest sinner, subdue the hardest heart, tame the wildest will, enlighten the darkest understanding, and break the strongest fetters. Thus, to quote Krummacher, the greatest evangelical preacher in Europe during the first half of the eighteenth century:

> To us the dying thief remains both an incomparable monument of the all-sufficiency of the blood of Christ, and a lofty candlestick on which the free grace of God beams as a flame, and an extremely significant beacon, yea, a lighthouse established by God for us on our passage through life. O, be assured that the spiritual footsteps of the dying malefactor with the words, *Remember me!* on his lips, points out to us this day the only path that points to Zion.

The Third Word of Love

LOVE THAT PROVIDES

"Woman, behold thy son! . . . Behold thy mother!"
John 19:26–27

Love That Provides

John Milton bids us remember that, "Freely we serve, because we freely love . . ." But love that fails to find service in the provision and thought of others has missed the way, for the mission of love is magnanimity. Further, to give to the limits without love, is profitless; true love never seeks its own (1 Cor. 13:3–5).

Jesus, Mary, and John, "the disciple whom Jesus loved," are superb and shining examples of love that serves and sacrifices for others. It was Mary who provided the body in which the holy child Jesus was to be fashioned. When the startling announcement reached her that she had been chosen to become the mother of our Lord, she said to Gabriel, "Be it unto me according to thy word." It was also Mary who, because of the deep love she bore for her first-born Son, provided for Him the love, comfort, and provision of the home in which He lived for thirty years. Yes, and it was Mary who stood by His cross, providing Him with necessary affection and sympathy when others had forsaken Him. In Gethsemane an angel appeared to strengthen Him, but now, He who took not on Him the nature of angels felt there was something still sweeter in the sympathy of the human love His mother displayed.

A precious aspect of the cross is the way the Lord Jesus, in the last hour of His agony, thought of His brave mother and of the vacancy His going would mean in her life. She was blessed among women because she became His mother, and the thoughtful provision He made for her future in the home of John proved His loving care of her. As for John who earned the coveted title of "The Apostle of Love," his love for the Lord led him to take Mary into his family circle and provide for her as a son for a bereaved mother. When he came to write his three epistles, love for others, actuated by the love of God in the heart, formed their principal theme. Those who close their eyes to surrounding need cannot have divine love indwelling them, for such love lives for the relief of others. To prove his point, John uses the somber illustration of Calvary where God the Son laid down His life to provide a world of sinners, lost and ruined by sin with a perfect salvation. Of true, selfless love, the poet Blake wrote:

> Love seeketh not itself to please
> Nor for itself hath any care;
> But for another gives its ease,
> And builds a Heaven in Hell's despair.

With this preamble in mind, then, let us consider how Jesus, Mary, and John are linked together in The Third Word of Love from the cross.

The first three words that Jesus uttered as He hung upon the cross, can be woven into an unbreakable threefold cord. In His First Word He embraced a world of sinners; in His Second Word He gathered His first fruits in the salvation of a stranger; in His Third Word He addressed His nearest and dearest. Having just provided a heavenly home for a penitent sinner, He now provides an earthly home for His widowed, sorrowing mother. The first utterance was a prayer for the forgiveness of the rabble crowd who had clamored for His death. The second utterance was for the felon at His side.

The third utterance in the magnanimous trilogy was on behalf of His mother and of John—utterances displaying pity, power, and provision. As Dr. James Stalker expressed it:

> The words He spoke were, indeed, few; but they completely covered the case. Every word He uttered in that position was with great pain; therefore He could not say much. Besides, their very fewness imparted to them a kind of judicial dignity; as has been said, this was Christ's last will and testament. To His mother He said, "Woman behold thy son!"—which can carry the sad meaning, "Woman, thou hast no son now." Then indicating John with His eyes, He merely said, "Behold thy mother!" It was simple, yet comprehensive; a plain, almost legal direction, and yet overflowing with love to both Mary and John.

Looking again at the first three of the Seven Words we can see that in life and in death Jesus executed the triple offices of prophet, priest, and king. His *first Word* from the cross was a priestly prayer of intercession, "Father, forgive them; for they know not what they do." His *second Word* was the royal promise of a king, "Today shalt thou be with me." His *third Word* revealed Him as the great prophet of humanity, "When Jesus therefore saw his mother, and the disciple standing by, whom he loved, he saith unto his mother, Woman behold thy son! Then saith he to the disciple, Behold thy mother! And from that hour that disciple took her unto his own home." Thus, as one writer puts it, "His love follows us *home.*" As the valley of the shadow of death approaches, "the energies of thought are taxed to the full by last farewells and messages of love to those who have been nearest and dearest."

From His cross, then, the Savior rained down legacies, and "no showers were ever so rich in harvests as the red drops of Calvary." In each of these last three words are gifts abiding and universal, particular as well as temporary. His first prayer was not merely for the crucifiers but for representatives of a larger company, even for you and me that we might experience the joy of forgiveness. Then for the thief there was the precious gift of paradise, bringing the promise and breath of Eden into every death chamber. And there was the special gift for His mother and for John, in which He gave John to Mary and Mary to John. The hour John took Mary into his own home was an hour singled out from other hours and marked the definite beginning of a new relation between the two. John took Mary, not only into his home but into his heart, making provision, thereby, for moral affinities of heart, thought, character, temperament, and faith.

A MOTHER LOSES HER SON

It is customary for us to speak of those near to us who die as being "lost." Thus, bereaved parents will say, "We have just lost our dear child." But, actually, this is not the language we should use of a believer. No person or possession is lost if we know where they are. Therefore, when loved ones in Christ come to the end of their earthly pilgrimage, we know where they are continuing their journey. Absent from the body, they are at home with the Lord. Not *lost* but *alive* forevermore. They have simply changed earth for heaven, and time for eternity.

There was a day when Mary did lose her twelve-year-old son, and for three days He was a missing person. Along with her husband, Mary hunted for the lad and found Him in the temple, only to learn that there was a way in which ultimately she was to lose her first-born forever. When Jesus said to His mother, "Wist ye not that I must be about my father's business?" she knew in her own incommunicable thoughts that she was to lose Him in order that He might bring many sons and daughters to Glory. True, He returned to Nazareth and was subject to Joseph and Mary and continued living in the home for another eighteen years, but all through those years Mary did not have, and enjoy, that sense of possession which means everything to a loving mother.

Soon after Jesus left His sheltered home and entered His brief but dynamic ministry there came the occasion of His first miracle when Mary asked Him for a favor only to be met with a seemingly harsh reply, "Woman, what have I to do with thee?" The prophetic sword pierced this mother's heart, as she realized that from now on she must slip into the shadows. When Mary attempted to use "a mother's passport" and tried to reach her son through others with the plea, "Behold thy mother seeks for thee," the reply she received seemed an outrage, "Who is my mother?"

The sword cut deeper into Mary's mother-heart when she knew that the death her son was dying was the death of a criminal. It is always hard for a loving mother to see a son of hers die, but what anguish is comparable to that of one watching her son enduring capital punishment prescribed for evil deeds? That mother at Calvary knew, however, that her son on that middle cross was the sinless One and was willing to die in every circumstance of disgrace and distress for those who were sinners. This thought must have helped to steady her soul in that dark hour. Knowing that her son was innocent and had always been pure, noble, and good, kept her calm when grief was most intense. Had He been guilty of the crimes laid against Him, and for which the authorities crucified Him, hers would have been a sorrow far worse than death. Her silent agony was intensified because she could do nothing to relieve her son's suffering in such a tragic hour. As James Stalker asks:

What mother's sufferings were ever equal to Mary's? There He hung before her eyes; but she was helpless. His wounds bled, but she dared not staunch them; His mouth was parched, but she could not moisten it. Those outstretched arms used to clasp her neck; she used to fondle those pierced hands and feet. Ah! the nails pierced her as well as Him; the thorns round His brow were a circle of flame about her heart; the taunts flung at Him wounded her likewise.

During a considerable portion of the time Jesus was suffering upon the cross, Luke says, "And all His acquaintance, and the women that followed Him from Galilee, stood afar off, beholding these things" (23:49). After nearly three hours of awful endurance, a small group ventured nearer the cross of Jesus. Along with John were believing women— Mary, the mother of Jesus; the two other Marys; the wife of Cleophas; Mary of Magdala—standing in close proximity beside the cross. Says Spurgeon, "Last at the Cross, First at the Sepulchre, no woman's lips betrayed her Lord; no woman's hand ever smote Him; their eyes wept for Him; they gazed upon Him with pitying awe and love. God bless the Marys! When we see so many of them about the Cross, we feel that we honour the very name Mary."

Chrysostom is credited with the saying that "the weaker sex on this occasion proves itself the stronger." Other believers forsook Him and fled, but these women were true to the last. One man and three women, perhaps four, if John's "Salome" was his mother (19:25), formed that little sorrowing company. The history of the church reveals that frequently faithful women show a greater devotion to their Lord than do men. One wonders what churches would do today without the loyal women who attend.

Conspicuous among the women at the cross was Mary, the mother of the One all were watching, and who had inner thoughts and anguish the others could not share. To the mob who heaped taunts upon the dying Christ, Mary appeared to be a humble, peasant woman of Galilee, whose north country accent betrayed her origin. Dr. S. J. Reid describes her:

> Her worn hands tell of a lifetime of household drudgery. Her dress tells of the poverty she had lived in since the day when she made an offering of two young pigeons at the circumcision of her Son. Her brow is furrowed, her hair is white, for the burden of over fifty years is upon her, and the lines of age and care which come so ungraciously and so early in the East, deepened by the added sorrows of widowhood, are marked upon her face and figure.

It was to this godly mother that Jesus turned in His dying hour. His last thoughts were of her, not with any thought of being comforted by her as she had often done when He was a child, but of her pain, and of her future once He was gone. His heart was a heart of flesh and His chivalrous manhood would not permit Him to forget the one who had brought Him into the world. Thus, "from the pulpit of His cross, Jesus preaches to all ages a sermon on the Fifth Commandment." The position and posture of His mother must have caught His eye, for we read, "Now there stood by the cross of Jesus his mother . . . when Jesus therefore saw his mother, and the disciple standing by, whom he loved, he saith unto his mother, Woman, behold thy son!" (John 19:25, 26).

We read of those who *sat* with stolid indifference and watched Him. Not so with Mary! She *stood!* Poets have found in Mary's station at the cross an appealing theme to express. Mary herself could have sung the expressive verses of E. C. Clephane's wonderful Calvary hymn, "Beneath the Cross of Jesus, I fain would take my stand." Then there are the lines of Henry Mills:

> Near the Cross was Mary weeping,
> There her mournful station keeping,
>   Gazing on her dying Son:
> There with speechless grief oppressèd
> Anguish-stricken and distressed.
>   Through her soul the sword had gone.

But while writers and hymnists describe Mary weeping so copiously and sorrowfully, the Gospels are silent as to a river of tears staining her anguish-stricken face as she gazed upon the blood-spattered form of her dying son. John says nothing about tears. There was no fainting, no paroxysm. True, through her heart the sword of agony was passing as with mother-instinct she felt His pains, and the grief of her own heart could not fail in touching her son's heart, for Mary had a mother's portion in the love of His heart—soon to be broken. What else can we do but marvel at her self-control, as she stands but does not sob or speak? She exhibited the great lessons of courage, fortitude, and faith learned from her son! Although He had passed in thought and experience far beyond her understanding, she could yet stand there, silent and loving, sharing his travail of soul.

The verb used for "stood," emphatic in word order, pluperfect in tense, implies that she had stood there from the outset of the act of crucifixion. Yet under the strain of standing so long she did not faint or collapse under the immense burden of her anguish, but in reverent dignity stood by her dying son. It would not have been natural if a gentle shower of tears had not dampened her cheeks, but no heart-sob proceeded from her lips, as in the case of others who smote their breasts as they beheld the sight of the One hanging on the tree in agony and shame. The portrait Taylor sketches of Mary in his *Exemplar*, Vol. 3, is worthy of repetition:

> By the Cross of Christ stood the holy virgin—mother, upon whom old Simeon's prophecy was now verified; for now she felt "a sword passing through her very soul." She stood without clamour, or womanish noises, and silent, and with a most deep grief as the waters of the abyss, but smooth as the face of a pool, full of love and patience, and sorrow and hope. Now she was put to it to make use of all those excellent discourses her holy Son had used to build up her spirit, and fortify it against this day. Now she felt the blessings and strengths of faith, and she passed from the grief of the Passion to the expectation of the Resurrection; and she rested in this death as in a sad remedy, for she knew it reconciled God with all the world.

Coming to our Lord's words to Mary, to which she listened in silence, we can consider them in this perspective: (1) What Jesus called his mother—*Woman!* (2) What he called himself—*Behold thy son!*

What he called his mother. In modern parlance, calling a female, *Woman*, does not convey much expression of honor or affection. What contempt there was in the voice of the Pharisee who said of a much-abused creature, *"This* woman . . ."* Alongside of this less intimate term John places the more familiar one of *mother*.

"He saith unto his mother, Woman, behold thy son!" (John 19:26). That motherhood was in the mind of Jesus when He addressed Mary as "Woman" is evidenced by the fact that He called upon her to behold Him as her son. As used in the Bible times, such a title implied no lack of respect or affection. Bishop Westcott, dealing with the use of "woman" by Jesus at the wedding feast at Cana wrote that "in the original there is not the least tinge of reproof or severity in the term. . . . It was the common title of respect."

Thus, although the language may sound strange in our ears as Jesus used it of His mother, it would be something of the equivalent of our designation, "Lady," a title of deference and honor. "Woman" was the word used by Hector in the tenderest scene of the *Iliad* when he bade farewell to his beloved wife, Andromachen, on the walls of Troy. A noticeable feature of our Lord's public life is the absence of any occasion when He called her "mother." Mary herself affirmed that she was His mother, and others referred to her as such. Because of the perfection of his character Jesus loved and honored Mary with perfect filial devotion, and in His earlier days must have often called her mother. But in all the brief conversations with her after He left home for His public ministry He never addressed her as such but always as "Woman," (John 2:4; 20:15; Luke 2:49). It would seem as if He always spoke to her in public with a certain air of restraint.

In fact, the way Jesus spoke to His mother seems to indicate an effort to tone down any popular conception of Mary, because of her filial relationship, having any special function in His kingdom (Matt. 12:46–50). Certainly, Mary knew that she was highly favored among women when chosen to become the mother of our Lord, but from that episode in the temple when He told her that henceforth He must be about His Father's business, she knew that in a very solemn sense a tie was to be broken as her son prepared to enter His ministry of reconciliation. She had to be reminded that, although His mother, she must not exercise any control over Him or interfere with Him as He fulfilled the divine mission His Father had sent Him into the world to accomplish. On one occasion Jesus put His mother on the same level as *all* who fulfill the will of God (Matt. 12:50; see also Luke 11:28). It has been said that the references in the Gospel memoirs as to expressions of tender affection between mother and son were "an inspired protest beforehand against the superstitions and idolatries of days that were to come."

Our Lord's public attitude toward His mother and His restraint in choice of words when in conversation with her discredit the claims of the Roman Church as to Mary being

"The Mother of God" . . . . "The Queen of Heaven." As
Jesus looked down from the cross on His mother, He saw her
as a sorrowing, heartbroken woman needing comfort, care,
and security, and He left her a legacy of a loving foster son
and his home.

Further, the title "Woman" indicated a ratification of that
repudiation of the earthly relationship Jesus made before
(Matt. 12:46–50). From henceforth, as the result of His
death, any person, even a penitent thief, is as close as Mary
in the realm of grace. And, let it not be forgotten that in her
Magnificat at the birth of her son, she confessed her need of
the saving grace He had come to manifest, for she sang, "My
spirit hath rejoiced in *God my Savior.*" At Calvary the full
revelation came to her that she must regard Jesus, not so
much as her son, but as the Savior of the world. "He had
been lifted up above that natural subjection to her as her
son which He so beautifully exemplified in the home at
Nazareth, and now she must take a lower rank under Him,
simply as one of His disciples." Thus she was found among
them after His resurrection (Acts 1:14), not above them, to
be prayed to, but one of them—praying *with* them. Krummacher's summary of what we have been discussing is most
helpful:

> It has been considered strange that the Saviour, in speaking to
> Mary, should have made use of the distant word, *Woman,*
> instead of the tender name of mother. In reply to this, it is
> certainly true that He did so, partly because He would not
> still more deeply wound her bleeding heart by the sweet title
> of mother, and likewise lest He should expose His mother to
> the rudeness of the surrounding crowd. But the chief reason
> why He used the more general term *Woman* lies much
> deeper, both in this and the well-known scene at the marriage
> in Cana. He certainly meant His mother to understand that
> henceforward His earthly connection with her must give way
> to a superior one. As though He had said, "Thou, My mother,
> wilt from this time be as one of My daughters, and I thy Lord.
> Thou believest in Me, and shalt be blessed. Thou layest hold
> of the hem of My garment, and I appear in thy stead. Thou
> adorest Me, and I am thy High Priest and King. Mother,
> brother, and sister, henceforward, are all who sware allegiance

to My banner. The relationship according to the flesh and the manner of the world have an end; other and more spiritual and heavenly take their place."

What he called himself. We will never fully understand all that was in the mind of Jesus when He said, "Behold thy Son!" nor all that filled the aching heart of the mother to whom these three poignant words were spoken. As the exclamation "Behold!" implies concentrated contemplation, an earnest looking at or an intent witness, it was a most gory spectacle Jesus called His mother to gaze upon. Naked, emaciated, and nail-pierced, there was certainly nothing attractive about him. Yet a devoted mother's loving eyes saw behind the blood and agony of her son, One who was the fairest of all.

In His previous Saying Jesus revealed His deity when He offered paradise to the penitent thief. Now, in His last message to His mother, He emphasizes the fact of His humanity—"Thy son." In this description of Himself Jesus confirms the Incarnation—that He came as God manifest in flesh. Christ the Lord was found lying in a cradle as Mary's firstborn son, whose name they called Jesus (Matt. 1:25; Luke 2:11, 12) and who, at the cross, bids His mother to look upon her son. He does not forget that He is her son, or that she is His dear and sorely-tried mother. With His compassionate heart, He knew what it meant for her to stand so resolutely and watch Him die in such agony and shame. Jesus was born of this now sorrowing woman and urges her to look upon Him, not as a helpless victim but as a mighty victor.

Our ideal of His perfect manhood would have been marred, if, in His dying hours, while speaking to and praying for others, Jesus had had no final word for the mother who had called herself "his handmaiden." In the midst of all Jesus was enduring in that dread hour He thought of her, who had been the guardian of His childhood and youth, and gave her as the inestimable legacy of love to His much-loved John. The injunction is to comfort widows in their affliction, and Mary was much afflicted as she stood by the cross—perhaps the only one of the family to witness the death of her son, she must have been greatly comforted as He makes every provision for her future security. The love, providing salvation by the cross was not unmindful of the material provision a bereaved widowed mother would need.

A Son Gains a Mother

Among the small, privileged circle made up of those the Gospels describe as being loved by Jesus was John who leaned on His bosom and who is repeatedly recognizable as "the disciple whom Jesus loved." With all modesty John was the disciple who wrote, "When Jesus therefore saw . . . the disciple standing by, whom he loved . . . Then saith he to the disciple, Behold thy mother! And from that hour that disciple took her unto his own home" (John 19:26–27). Transferring his gaze from His mother's face to the benign and loving face of John, Jesus gave him a gift of the mother who was losing her son. Because of His extreme anguish He might not have seen Mary and John near His cross, but in spite of His agonizing pain of heart and mind, thoughtfulness was supremely manifested in His word of comfort to His mother and in His instruction to His beloved disciple concerning her future.

The love of Calvary, being the love that provides, arranged mutual comfort for two who were to complement each other. Mary was to be to John a mother, and he was to be to her a loving son. The last act of Jesus before He died was to see that she had a roof over her head for the rest of her days. Jesus committed to His best friend the deepest treasure of His love—His mother! Thus His consideration and thoughtfulness, even in travail of soul, were perfect. Now, John must take His place and do for Mary what Jesus had done—to be to her what He had been. Archbishop Marcus L. Loane of Sydney has this enlightening comment on the action of Jesus:

John himself was first cousin to his Master, but this word from the Cross would make him a kinsman of still nearer standing. It would create the tie where it did not exist before, and would proclaim him a brother by bonds that were stronger than blood. It would recognize a mother's right to the love of her first-born; and would establish a kinsman's right to the place of a brother. Perhaps this is implied in the contrast between the term *woman* which He employed in His word to Mary and the term *mother* which He now used in His word to John. It was as though He wished John to take the word which He would not allow on His own lips, and we can sense His wish in the inflection which seems to underlie this brief phrase, "Behold thy *mother*."

As Mary had other sons and was not homeless, the question arises: Why did Jesus call upon His mother to look at Him as if He alone was her son, and why did He arrange for her to leave her own home and find one with John? We totally reject the assumption that Mary, who was a virgin when the Holy Spirit overshadowed her making possible "that Holy Thing" born of her, remained a virgin and never had other children. Certainly Jesus was Mary's first-born, but after her marriage to Joseph, other children came into the Nazareth home along the avenue of natural generation. There were James and Joses, Jude and Simon, and at least two sisters (Matt. 13:55, 56; Mark 6:3). But Jesus passed by these natural guardians after the death of the first-born and called attention to a disciple for the sacred office of caring for His mother about to be bereaved of her son.

Further, the tenor of Gospel references to the Nazareth family is against the idea held by some expositors that the other children mentioned were Joseph's by an earlier marriage and that the passage "Behold thy son!" implies that Mary herself had no other son of her own. Nothing could be plainer than the witness of those who were amazed at the miracles of Jesus, "His brothers, James and Joses, and Simon, and Judas. And his sisters, are they not with us?" (Matt. 13:55, 56). "Behold thy mother and thy brothers stand without, desiring to speak with thee" (Matt. 12:47–50).

Why, then, were not any of the other children named by Jesus, and why was Mary not placed in their care? The answer may be found in the declaration, "Neither did His brothers believe in Him" (John 7:5). None of His brothers and sisters are spoken of as being at the cross. Mary alone witnessed His death. Was she the only one in the family who believed that the dying One was indeed the Messiah, the Savior of the world? Thus, when Jesus said, "Woman, behold thy son!" He could have meant that He was the only one of her sons to believe that He had been manifested to destroy the works of the devil. Further, when Jesus told John to make his home, Mary's, He wanted His mother to have a godly home, such as she might not find among her other sons. Deeper spiritual ties were more important to Jesus than mere earthly relationships (Matt. 12:46–50; 2 Cor. 5:16). This we do know, that the other sons of Mary came to be believers, perhaps saved as the result of the death and resurrection of their elder brother, Jesus, for we find them numbered among the disciples awaiting Pentecost (Acts 1:14).

Loving and faithful John fulfilled Jesus' solemn trust, for he not only took Mary into his home but into his heart. Krummacher observes that the expression, "That disciple took her into his own home," implies, according to the original, "Much more than that he only took care of her in his habitation. He received her into his heart. It may easily be supposed what love he felt toward her from that time, and with what tenderness and fidelity he accompanied her through life. And because John's love was in reality no other than a sacred spark from Jesus' own breast, Mary was beloved by John, as before, with the love of her divine Son." John became a son to Mary in place of the One who died, and he learned to love as his mother her who had been the devoted mother of the One John had loved.

It was a token of the confidence Jesus had in His disciple when He committed His sorely-tried mother to John's care, and it must have been a lasting comfort to him to know that he had his Master's confidence. Then it is not difficult to imagine that John and Mary became kindred spirits, especially as they were one in their intense love for Jesus. How could they ever tire speaking to one another about Him? As James Stalker puts it, "Jesus honoured both of them in each other's eyes by giving them to one another in this way.

If He gave Mary a great gift in giving her John for a son, He gave him no less a gift by giving him such a mother; for Mary could not but be an ornament to any home." At the cross John received a sacred charge—to take the place of Jesus as a son in the life of His mother, and it was discharged to the limit.

Tradition has it that Mary enjoyed the loving shelter and hospitality of John's home for twelve years. As time went by, we can imagine how John came to call Mary, "Mother!" and how she would tenderly call John, "son!" with the ever present remembrance in both of their hearts to Him who had knit them together in one communion and fellowship. Love to Jesus made their hearts as one. Further, through the long-continued sojourn of Mary with John, the latter must have learned much from the former about the Incarnation and early life of Jesus. The assistance John received from Mary enabled him to write his Gospel about the Word becoming flesh. Archbishop Alexander would have us know that

> Mothers are the best biographers of their children's earlier years. They have a subtle insight, almost prophetic instincts. Who can doubt that the Annunciation, the Birth, the sweet silence of the baby and boy life, form a part of Mary's contribution to the materials of the authentic Gospels? . . . The heart of Mary had not been without influence on the hand of John.

One writer suggests that when Jesus said to Mary, "Behold thy son!" He did not mean that she was to view His piteous form on the cross, bleeding and dying, but that the two sayings, "Woman, behold thy son" and "Behold thy mother" are related to each other—that the disciple and the woman are the son and mother. According to this idea, in effect, Jesus said, "Behold one another, as son and mother"; seeing both Mary and John had already beheld Him as the Lamb of God taking away the sin of the world, and that both were to withdraw from the sight of His physical agonies and attend to their mutual duties in relation to one another as son and mother. I find it difficult, however, to accept this interpretation of the Third Word of Love from the cross.

Among the instructive features of the episode involving Jesus, Mary, and John, we can store up in our minds are, first of all, the consideration of others in their time of need. In His previous Word, Jesus taught that generosity is the remedy for selfishness in *prosperity*. Now, in this Third Word, He shows that consideration for others is the remedy against selfishness in *adversity*. Our Lord's consideration and thoughtfulness for others in need and suffering is conspicuous in His public ministry. His was ever a selfless love. Hubert Simpson would have us remember that "there are times when it may still be given to a trusted disciple to take the very place of Christ beside a troubled soul. It is the highest reward that life can command to become a bearer of the very comfort of God to a broken spirit in the hour of need or sorrow."

The second lesson we can take to heart, especially in these days of callous parental neglect, is that of obedience to the fifth commandment, "Honour thy father and thy mother." Even on the cross Jesus obeyed this command in a perfect manner. Not only was He subject to His parents in His youth, but as He dies, Jesus provides for Mary, leaving her a rich legacy of love. All sons and daughters should reflect upon the final act of Jesus for His mother. Even in the midst of the greatest sacrificial act the world has ever witnessed, the concern of the One dying was for the woman chosen to bring Him into the world that He might die for its salvation. Has He not left us an example that we should follow? Paul tells us that, "If a man provide not for his own, he hath denied the faith, and is worse than an infidel" (1 Tim. 5:8). Although dying for the world's spiritual needs, Jesus was not unmindful of Mary's temporal provision.

Widows and orphans can take note of the wider range of the cross, namely, that the Savior has their temporal as well as their spiritual and eternal interests at heart; that as they cast all their care upon Him, they can have assurance that He cares for them. Calvary confirms that Jesus can be as "a husband to the widow" and "bless the charities of home." As we lovingly linger at the cross and think of the future of Mary, Jesus provided for in the home of John, we are re minded of the still greater home-gift from the cross He promised His own a few days before: "In My Father's house are many mansions. . . . I go to prepare a place for you" (John 14:2). In the darkening hours of death when earthly home ties are broken, Jesus assures us of a home of redeemed hearts in a land where there is no death.

The Fourth Word of Love

LOVE THAT QUESTIONS

"My God, my God, why hast thou forsaken me?"
Matthew 27:46

Love That Questions

Tennyson, in "The Charge Of The Light Brigade," wrote of the six hundred who rode fearlessly out to the Valley of Death:

> Theirs not to reason why,
> Theirs but to do and die.

But Jesus did ask the reason *why* He had been forsaken of God as He died such an agonizing death. Because of their love for each other Jesus questioned His Father's desertion, seeing He had called Him His well-beloved Son. Dr. Joseph Parker, the famous expositor and pastor of the City Temple, London, during the latter half of the eighteenth century suffered a severe blow when his much-loved wife died most suddenly. His large congregation wondered what their pastor would preach about on the first Sunday after his dear one's burial. Dr. Parker took as his text the Fourth Word of the cross and began his sermon by saying that he was so grateful in the hour of his deep grief that there was a *why* in the heart and on the lips of Jesus as He came to die.

"My God, my God, why hast thou forsaken me?" Our finite minds will never be able to penetrate the full significance of these heart-rending words as Jesus died bearing the terrible load of human sin. Who can penetrate the broken heart of Jesus in the hour when everything joined to His agony of spirit? His acute physical pain, with its hideous nausea, the darkness blotting out the sight even of those who love Him, and, far worse, the realization of the abysmal evil of the burden of sin He was bearing for mankind. About those three hours of intense, terror-filled darkness nothing is said. Lips were sealed. Therefore, how can we penetrate the significance of such a period? Meditating upon the cry escaping the lips of Jesus as He emerged from such darkness, sacriligious curiosity and unholy intrusion, will not unveil the secret of all He suffered of divine justice as He became the bearer of the sin of the world. The middle saying of the cross forces us on our faces before God. As Dr. G. Campbell Morgan states it in his remarkable study, *The Crises of the Christ:*

> At the commencement of this study I would place it on record, not idly and not for mere sake of doing so, but under the urgency of a great conviction, that I am deeply conscious of approaching things too high, and too profound for any finality of statement.

It is with such a sentiment in mind that we approach our survey of the Fourth Word of Love, which is so startling and appalling in its implication. Those who heard such a bitter, terrible cry coming out of the darkness would never forget its tones for the rest of their days. Bishop J. Ryle would have us know that "there is a deep mystery in these words which no man can fathom. They express the real pressure on His soul of the enormous burden of the world's sin."

Surely no human cry of mercy has ever exceeded the one before us, yet, although it is associated with our Lord's deepest agony and unutterable woe and we will never fully understand all it means, it is recorded for our learning and by the Spirit we can know what it teaches. As the cry of One, who came to the edge of an overwhelming despair with a feeling that He is sinking into the dark abyss of death, the words are "familiar to the world at large in virtue of their repetition down the centuries, but they still form the most appalling utterance that has ever fallen upon human ears." We find ourselves confessing with Krummacher, "My soul trembles at the idea of approaching the unfathomable depth of suffering, from whence the cry of *Eli, Eli lama sabachthani* proceeded. How much rather would I lie prostrate on my face in silence before this awful incident, than write or speak upon it." No other cry has ever pierced the atmosphere of the earth than this which Jesus uttered with a loud voice and which must have caused a cold shudder of terror on the part of those who heard it. Down the centuries preachers and theologians have found the Fourth Word from the cross one of the most difficult in all the Bible to explain and expound. Yet, as James Stalker reminds us, "There is great reward in grappling with such difficult passages; for never does the truth impress us so profoundly as when we are made to feel that all the length which we are able to go is only into the shallows of the shore, while beyond our reach lies the great ocean."

A fact to observe is that this was *the only* last word at Calvary to be recorded by the first two Evangelists, Matthew (27:45–46) and Mark (15:33–34), in their report of the crucifixion, which suggests something of the profound impression it must have had upon these writers. Further, the central position this last word holds in the Seven Words that were uttered is worthy of notice and full of interest. In the ordered sequence of the Seven Words, the central one is related most intimately to the most mysterious crisis of all in the drama of our redemption. The first Three Words were connected with the needs of others, while the last Three Words are all related to the need and accomplishment of Jesus. But in the Fourth Word Jesus passes from the circle of those around Him to the center of all, namely, what He endured during the three hours of total darkness. All last Four Words, of course, reveal how absorbed He was in His own concerns.

It is, then, to his own concern, namely, the conscious sense of being God-forsaken, that we now give our solemn and prayerful attention. As darkness and desertion are linked together, both by Matthew and Mark, in almost identical language, we cite the connected passages: "Now from the sixth hour there was darkness over all the land (Mark: 'over the whole land') unto the ninth hour. And about the ninth hour Jesus cried with a loud voice, saying, Eli, Eli, lama sabachthani? that is to say, My God, my God, why hast thou forsaken me?"

We may find it profitable to apply the telescopic method to our meditation of this passage, drawing it out section by section.

There Was Darkness Over the Whole Land

After the first Three Words which, in all likelihood, were uttered in quick succession, there followed a prolonged period of mysterious darkness and eerie silence. If, after Jesus' conversation with Mary and John, the phrase "From that hour that disciple took her unto his home" means that they left the cross for John's home nearby, then they were both spared the terror of the hours of darkness as well as the anguished cry of Jesus. A change came over the grim scene at Calvary. For, as in the ancient plague of Egypt, a thick darkness which could be felt stole over the heavens and hid all things from men's eyes, so as Jesus died, black darkness covered the land and out of it came the bitter cry of dereliction from Him who was suffering on the middle cross.

From the sixth hour to the ninth hour, or, according to our time from twelve noon to 3 o'clock in the afternoon, a strange pall of gloom shadowed the land and midday became as black as midnight. This was not "an eclipse, for the full moon cannot come between the earth and the sun. It was not like nightfall, for the moon did not shine as it usually did." Luke's brief detail affords a vivid picture, "And the sun was darkened" (23:45). But how? At whose command did the sun refuse to look on such a deed of shame men had perpetrated in the crucifixion of the naked sufferer on the cross? The three Evangelists mentioning this weird phenomenon (Matt. 47:45; Mark 15:33; Luke 23:44) all seem to indicate that in some sense nature was in sympathy with her Lord. Without doubt, "by some preordained harmony, the darkness was in sympathy with the anguish of the dying Lord of Heaven and Earth."

Mark tells us that it was the third hour when Jesus was nailed to the cross, and three hours from sunrise would be about 9 o'clock in the morning (Mark 15:25). This means that Jesus from 9 o'clock until noon endured the glaring sun as He suffered the continuing and increasing pain of crucifixion. Priests and people alike exposed Him to taunts of vulgar insult. He had been left to die in naked need and disgrace. Then something strange happened as light fled the sky and darkness covered the land and His cross. Job wrote of those who "meet with darkness in the daytime, and grope in the noonday as in the night" (5:14). This must have been the experience of many in the vicinity of Calvary the day Jesus died there. Just the night before his crucifixion Jesus had said to the chief priests and elders and captains of the Temple, "This is your hour and the power of darkness" (Luke 22:53). But even with that they were amazed at midnight darkness at midday.

Because there is always something mysterious about darkness, people are usually afraid of it. The degree and nature of the unusual darkness at the cross are not defined. We are not told whether it came gradually or with dramatic suddenness. Of one thing we are certain, though: it was not natural but supernatural. The Psalmist speaks of God making "darkness His secret place" (Ps. 18:11), and Calvary's darkness was His act. "The sun did not obscure itself, but it was the Almighty Who clothed it in that mourning-dress." As darkness and light are both alike to God, the terrible phenomenon at the cross was the finger of the Almighty.

Moses tells us how God thundered out of the "thick darkness, with a great voice" (Deut. 5:22), but the darkness at Calvary brought about a marked change in the conduct of those gathered there. Silence reigned during that three-hour pause. Gibes and taunts ceased. No sound came from man, not even from Christ Jesus. "He opened not his mouth." Whatever may have passed between Father and Son during that reign of darkness "lies for the present sealed with seven seals, hidden in the depths of Eternity." It was only as darkness gave way to light that Jesus broke the uncanny silence of those three hours and cried, *"Eli, Eli, lama sabachthani?"*

Isaiah speaks of "the treasures of darkness" (45:3). Perhaps the darkness surrounding the cross was precious in that it was inanimate nature showing her sympathy with the Lord of nature. An unusual star shone at His birth—a miraculous cloud at His transfiguration—now, just before His death, there is a period of mysterious darkness as a protest on the part of nature against man's cruel treatment of Jesus. The Scottish preacher, Robert Gilchrist, has pointed out the striking contrast between the birth and the death of our Lord:

> The sun was darkened at *noon,* and Christ was crucified in His prime. At His birth the glory of the Lord shone round the shepherds of Bethlehem in the field by night, and the angels sing, "Glory to God in the highest, and on earth peace, goodwill toward men." At His death there is no light but darkness; no song but silence. He was born in the night, and in the night there was a supernatural light. He was crucified in the day, and in the day there was a supernatural darkness. Yet the day of His death was better than the day of His birth.

The symbolic significance of the darkness which shielded Jesus from the mob who sat down to watch Him die has been summarized for us in the Calvary hymn of Isaac Watts:

> Well might the sun in darkness hide,
>   And shut His glories in,
> When Christ, the mighty Maker, died,
>   For man the creature's sin.

Such darkness was the evidence of God's judgment on sin, as well as the symbol of the deeper darkness, even the "outer darkness" where there is the eternal weeping and gnashing of teeth. "The Lord was on the cross as the Bearer of sin; He was in the place where judgment must fall. The smile of God's love was withdrawn when the sun hid its light; the frown of God's wrath was revealed when day turned to night. Darkness over all the land was a sign of the eclipse of God's face while sin was being judged and exposed." The Psalmist says, "The darkness hideth not from thee" (139:12), yet, in some mysterious way in the darkness at the cross, God was hid from His only begotten Son.

No words can fully express what transpired during those three awful hours because no finite mind can imagine all the Savior endured during them, save that the outer darkness typified and illustrated an inner darkness culminating in His cry of desolation. Reverently, touching the fringe of this great mystery, we can say that the darkness over all the land symbolized the hiding of the consciousness of the Father's presence from the human soul of Jesus. As He bore our sins in His own body on the cross, Jesus was made to experience the essential separation caused by sin. Before He shouted in triumph, "It is finished!" He was being made sin—not a sinner—for us. During those dark hours sin in some unknown way took possession of all His human faculties, and He paid the penalty of sin by His death. The loudness of His cry revealed the intensity of His anguish as it came from One who knew He was tasting the dark abyss of death for every sinner (Heb. 2:9, 14, 15). Death and the curse were in His cup.

There is another application we can make of the darkness covering the whole land. It was a type of the whole world lost in the darkness of sin and of all living within the world being blinded by the god of the world. John reminds that men love darkness rather than light because their deeds are evil; that Jesus came as the Light to shine in the darkness of the world but that the darkness comprehended it not (John 1:1–14). At Calvary it seemed as if the nocturnal darkness had extinguished Jesus, the Light of the world, but, as our further meditation will prove, it was just in His vicarious death that the light of salvation and of eternal life rose upon a dark world.

Ye dwellers in darkness, with sin-blinded eyes,
   The Light of the world is Jesus:
Go, wash at His bidding, and light will arise,
   The Light of the world is Jesus.

In approaching a study of the language Jesus used in his Fourth Word from the cross, there are three introductory matters to consider, the first being the physical causes of the cry. The Savior Christ was truly man, and because of the perfection of His humanity must have felt pain more acutely than His companions in crucifixion. What meditations were His during the three hours of anguish we are not told, but the cry with which He broke the silence of this period may be taken as an index of His mental state throughout it. It was a cry out of the lowest depths of despair, and was completely different from His habitual mood. What presently concerns us is the physical element associated with the cry.

From the moment Jesus was nailed to the cross He was in considerable pain, and every moment the agony increased. As James Stalker describes the torture:

> The wounds in His hands and feet, exposed to the atmosphere and the sun, grew barked and hardened; the blood, impeded in its circulation, swelled in heart and brain, till these organs were like to burst; and the slightest attempt to move the body from one intolerable posture caused pains to shoot along the quivering nerves. Bodily suffering clouds the brain and distorts the images formed on the mirror of the mind. Even the face of God, reflected there, may be turned to a shape of terror by the fumes of physical trouble. The horror of mortal suffering may have been greater to Jesus than to other men, because of the fineness and sensitiveness of His physical organization.

The longer Jesus stayed upon the cross, the more the unity of His perfect nature was being violently torn asunder. Yet it was through the rent veil of His flesh that the way was opened to enter the presence of the holiest of all. Jesus drained the cup to its dregs. No angel was sent to rescue or strengthen Him. His heavenly Father interposed with no miracle to deliver Him from so great a death. Heaven

abandoned Him to His dread fate. But although we may
not know the pains He bore, yet the glorious truth is that
"the five bleeding wounds He bears . . . pour effectual
prayers" on our behalf.

The second thought to briefly dwell upon is the timing
of Christ's Fourth Word which came, not during the silent,
sorrowful three-hour period but at the close of such an appalling and agonizing experience. The Sufferer breaks His
long silence with a cry of distress, as if from the shaft of a
mine, and like a trumpet-sound of victory the incomprehensible and heart-affecting exclamation breaks forth, "Eli,
Eli, lama sabachthani?" Under the influence of reverential
awe, the Evangelists give us this cry in the same language in
which it was uttered. It is as if they were apprehensive lest a
rendering of it into Greek might detract somewhat from its
import.

The original casts the cry not in the form of a present but
as a past experience. Thus, the RV margin reads, "My God,
my God, why didst thou forsake me?" Phillips translation
reads, "My God, my God, why did you forsake me?" Canon
Peter Green, commenting on the past tense, says, "We may
believe that this is rather a cry of wonder at a torture now
past, an expression of amazed relief now the sense of His
Father's presence is restored, than the cry of agony of One
who is at the time, shut out from God's presence." The sun
was shining again in all its glory when Jesus cried, "Why
didst thou forsake me?" As Jesus uttered this cry, the past
hours of darkness were over, and He was basking again in
unclouded light. The overwhelming feeling of desertion
was over and gone, lying in the distance, "Why *didst* Thou?"

The third aspect of the cry is that of prophetic fulfillment.
In the hours of His sharpest grief Jesus turned to the
Psalms He dearly loved to find a fit utterance for His anguish
of soul, and He found it in the opening words of Psalm 22,
which He quoted verbatim. The acts of the soldiers in
gambling for His garments (Ps. 22:18 with Matt. 27:35) and
the taunts of His enemies about His Father being able to
deliver Him (Ps. 22:8 with Matt. 27:43) made this ancient
Psalm so real to Jesus as the prophetic description of all

He was enduring that He knew Scripture was being fulfilled by His gruesome death. As He emerged from the shadows He may have quoted the first line of the Psalm in order to direct the thoughts of those near the cross to the great messianic prophecy the Psalm contains. In making the Psalmist's cry of misery His own, Jesus declared Himself to be, as the Living Word, the embodiment of the Written Word. Other saints exhibited the instantaneous succession of the sense of abandonment and of intensest faith (Job 19:6–9; 23–26; Jeremiah 20:7–9, 12, 13). If conscious, as we come to the end of our pilgrimage, may our last word be that of a divine promise, precious to our hearts throughout life.

Neil M. Fraser provides us with the serviceable outline:

The Period—"At the ninth hour."

The evening sacrifice was at the ninth hour—three in the afternoon, a period and ordinance heavy with portentous happenings, propitious with impending blessings.

The Power—"Jesus cried with a loud voice."

Like the Passover lamb, a male of the first year, Jesus died in the fullness of His strength. In spite of His extreme pain there was no waning of His vocal powers.

The Price—"My God, my God, why hast thou forsaken me?"

What a price He paid for salvation! The price of our forgiveness was His forsakenness. The price of our nearness to God was the turning of God from Jesus as He bore the load of our sin. It is to an understanding of the tremendous cost of redemption that we now give ourselves. May the Holy Spirit take up the truth concerning all that is compressed in this cry from the cross and reveal it unto us!

My God, My God!

This poignant cry, though an utterance of despair, yet involved the strongest faith, for with both hands Jesus laid hold of God with whom He had been from the beginning (John 1:1). Actually, the repeated phrases were a prayer, and daily Jesus had turned to this divine resource in times of trial and stress and does so now in the hours of His supreme need and suffering. Says Spurgeon, "Our Lord's faith did not for a moment falter, for He says twice, '*My* God, *my* God.' O, the mighty double grip of His unhesitating faith! He seems to say, 'Even if Thou hast forsaken Me, I have not forsaken Thee.' Faith triumphs, and there is no sign of any faintness of heart towards the living God." Repeated words or phrases imply divine emphasis and establishment. Krummacher's comment on the repetition, *My God,* is most helpful:

Jesus makes it evident that solely by means of His naked faith He had struggled through all opposing feelings; and that God was still His God. Does He not, in the repetition, still cling with filial fondness to His heavenly Father, and say—although the words, "My God," instead of "My Father," leave us to infer a superiority of inward reverence in the presence of Eternal Majesty—"Between Thee and Me there can never be any separation!"

Then, is not the repeated *My*—the pronoun of personal possession—significant? Jesus did not cry "O God," but "*My* God," for he was still, as always, *My* God. Deep suffering has one of two effects upon the human soul. It either sours and embitters and drives it away from God or else makes it loving and tender and gentle and brings it closer to God. The gloom of desolation enveloped Jesus, yet He clung to God. Although God was laying upon His Son the iniquity of us all, yet He cleaves to the Father as His God. Stricken, smitten of God, and afflicted, the Son with unfaltering loyalty looks up to Him permitting such travail of soul and stays Himself upon the Lord as His God. Forsaken, yet unshaken!

It is not easy to turn to the hand smiting us, yet Jesus set us an example in His cry which was not *against* God but *to* God. Heart and flesh failed, yet He could still pray, "My God, My God." As Spurgeon observes:

The grip of appropriation is in the word *My,* but the reverence of humility is in the word *God.* It is "My *God,*" "*My* God." Thou art ever God to Me. Thy rights are unquestioned, for

Thou art My *God*. Thou canst do as Thou Wilt, and I yield
to Thy sacred sovereignty. I kiss the hand that smites Me, and
with all My heart cry *"My God, My God!"*

Emerging from the dense darkness of three hours Jesus is
still clasping and is clasped in the arms of God. At the most
terrible moment of His anguish God was still His God. Have
we not need to pray that we may follow our Savior and never
miss God in the dark but rather press closer to Him, sus-
tained by His favor and finally delivered through His grace?
If you had one anchor before, cast out two anchors, and
double the hold of your faith. *My* God, *my* God. *My God*
was not the usual way Jesus addressed him. *Father, my
Father* were His frequent expressions. But on the cross He
was bearing the condemnation a righteous God has pronounced upon sinners, and such a thrice holy God, hating
sin, was *His* God.

The repeated phrase, then, is not an expression of doubt,
but a prayer of faith, for no man can cry *"my* God" who is
without God in the world. As James Stalker expresses it, "No
one is forsaken who can pray, 'My God.' As one in deep
water, feeling no bottom, makes a despairing plunge forward
and lands on solid ground, so Jesus, in the very act of uttering His despair, overcame it. Feeling forsaken of God, He
rushed into the arms of God; and these arms closed around
Him in loving protection. Accordingly, as the darkness,
which had brooded over the land, disappeared at the ninth
hour, so His mind emerged from eclipse; and, as we shall see,
His last words were uttered in His usual mood of serenity."

Why?

Human reason will never be able to explain the mystery of
the cross. While in the flesh, man will ever see through a
glass darkly. We will never be able to fully understand all
that was involved when Jesus died that we might be forgiven and that at last we might go to heaven saved by His
precious blood. Why Jesus felt forsaken as He procured our
forgiveness is beyond our ken. Love that questions is not
love that doubts; a love ready to follow God, even in any

darkness, will prevail. *Why,* this middle word of the middle cry from the cross, is one we all use in times of anguish and perplexity. But coming from the lips of Jesus it seems contrary to His former complete acquiescence with the will of God. James Stalker says that the intellectual character of the pain of Jesus is indicated by His *Why.*

All the contradictions and confusions of the World were focussed on Golgotha. Injustice was triumphant, innocence was scorned and crushed, everything was exactly the reverse of what it ought to have been. And all the millions of *Whys* which have risen from agonized souls, jealous for the honour of God, but perplexed by His providence, were concentrated in the *Why* of Christ.

While we cannot probe the heart of the Master's *why* or plumb its depths of nameless agony, He, Himself, in His inmost being, knew why the sense of temporary desertion had been His experience. Because, however, His manhood was being crushed, distorted, humiliated, and subjected to excruciating pain and suffering, for a moment, "the finite soul of the Man Christ Jesus came into awful contact with the infinite justice of God . . . and He used language which is all too hot with anguish to be dissected by the cold hand of a logical criticism . . . a language which only the ear of sympathy can fully receive."

Do you not think that the questioning One would have us meditate upon the *why* and wherefore of His grief and mark the gracious motive for its endurance? He was dying as the sinless Substitute for sinners, and as such He had to endure distance and desolation because these are the inevitable consequences of sin which ever separate from God. The measure, then, of the Savior's *why* is the measure of human guilt and the measure of divine holiness. David, who penned the Psalm from which the cry is taken, gave the answer to his *why.* "Why hast thou forsaken me? . . . thou art holy" (Ps. 22:1–3). The cross vindicates the outraged holiness of God and provides the grace and salvation whereby the vilest sinner can enter the holiest of all.

Further, the *why* of Jesus proves how He entered into and can now sympathize with all the perplexities which beset human life. When He cried, "My God, my God, *why?*" He echoed forth the cry of mystified and distressed saints of all ages. Every age produces its own moral chaos and disasters and disorders, involving human life with a force it cannot understand, and there rises to heaven innumerable importunate questionings, "Why is thy wrath so hot against the sheep of thy pasture? Why hast thou cast us off?"

Job, supreme among mortal men as a sufferer, has given us a book full of *whys* and *wherefores*. In fact his voice sounds like that of a blasphemer when he cries, "Why did I not die from the womb? Why did I not give up the ghost when I came out of the belly?" Jeremiah is another who cried *why* and *wherefore* to God in terms of startling boldness. "Wherefore doeth the Lord our God all these things unto us? Wherefore doth the way of the wicked prosper?"

It has been pointed out that "callous minds learn to be content without explanations," and that "the ignorant, the frivolous and the time-serving are safe from" any *whys;* for they are well enough satisfied with things as they are. It is always painful, however, when a godly creature has to say *why* to his Creator. Are we not grateful, therefore, when perplexity fills our mind, that Jesus was made in all points like unto His brethren even in asking *why?* All of us live under "the discipline of ignorance," and fail to give a complete and satisfactory answer to the questions we ask.

Have you never been driven to say, "My God, *why?*" Why has God permitted loss of health or wealth or allowed sorrow, heartache, and tragedy to mar my happiness? Why does God seem indifferent to the glaring sins; crimes, and violence of our times? As the Creator, why does He not stay the forces of nature when they set out to destroy countless numbers of innocent lives in earthquakes, tornadoes, volcanoes, and floods? Why does God not keep men from making wars and indulging in misery and massacres? The Psalmist, because of his tears and trials, was taunted by his friends, "Where is thy God?" Was He dead or indifferent? So he asked his perplexed spirit, "Why art thou cast down, O my

soul? Why art thou disquieted within me?" Then he gives
the medicine for his malady: Hope thou in God! (Ps. 42).
At present we may see through a glass darkly but the day
is coming when God will unroll the canvas and explain the
reason why the dark days were as needful as the bright days
in life. Let it not be forgotten that Calvary's Sufferer who
cried, *"Why* hast thou forsaken me?" was the One who Himself declared, "What I do, thou knowest not now, but thou
shalt know hereafter."

> Not now, but in the coming years—
>   It may be in the better land—
> We'll read the meaning of our tears,
>   And there, some time, we'll understand
>
> We'll catch the broken threads again,
>   And finish what we here began;
> Heaven will the mysteries explain,
>   And then, ah then, we'll understand.
>
> We'll know why clouds instead of sun
>   Were over many a cherished plan;
> Why song has ceased when scarce begun;
>   'Tis there, some time, we'll understand.
>
> Why what we long for most of all
>   Eludes so oft our eager hand,
> Why hopes are crushed, and castles fall—
>   Up there, some time, we'll understand.

THOU!

It is not hard to imagine the emphasis Jesus gave to this
personal pronoun of the second person singular, as He uttered it on the cross, "Why didst *thou*—thou, my heavenly
Father above all others, forsake me?" Calvary would not have
been so hard to bear if Jesus had only felt the presence of
His Father with Him during those three hours of terrible
darkness both around and within Him. David, describing
his experience when the terrors of death had fallen upon
him, confesses that the horror overtaking him would not
have been so terrible to endure if only those professing to be
fellow-pilgrims to the house of God had not contributed to

his sorrow and soreness of heart: "For it was not an enemy that reproached me; then I could have borne it: neither was it he that hated me that did magnify himself against me; then I would have hid myself from him: But it was thou, a man mine equal, my guide, and mine acquaintance" (Ps. 55:12–13) .

What heart-break and poignancy are crammed into David's *thou,* and was it not so with David's Greater Son when He said to God with whom He was co-equal, *"Thou* hast forsaken me?"* Jesus predicted that His disciples would desert Him, but His confidence was "Yet I am not alone, for the father is with me." Yet a few hours later, as He dies upon the cross, He experiences the bitterness of being forsaken by His Father and cries, "Why hast *thou* left me alone?" The divine Presence He had basked in all along was now withdrawn from Him in the hour of greatest need. Such a stroke cut Jesus to the quick, for this was no phantom of the gloom but a real absence which He mourned.

The tone of this Fourth Word was that of astonishment that such an event could happen. If Jesus was "sore amazed" in Gethsemane, He was more so at Golgotha. Men might forsake Him, but how could God, His Father, leave Him in the lurch? James Stalker says that the same kind of accentuation of the *thou* is akin to the word with which the murdered Caesar fell: "Et *tu* Brute?"— *Thou* also Brutus? Whenever Jesus found Himself rejected of men or suffering treason and betrayal, as He did at the hands of Judas, He was always able to turn away from those who had deserted Him and cast Himself with confidence on the breast of God. But now in the hour of His most acute suffering that loving breast is no longer near for Him to find comfort on. The God who had sent an angel to console Him in Gethsemane, leaves His Son in the darkness alone.

Has not the pang, "Why hast *thou* forsaken me?" escaped many a human heart deserted by lover and friend? Are there not multitudes of hearts, broken by the desertion or deceit of close and trusted friends, who have found consolation in their forsakenness by turning to the cross on which the Lord Christ asked out of a broken heart, "Why hast *thou* forsaken me?" The glory of the gospel is that He was left alone, forsaken of His Father that He might be able to promise his redeemed children, "I will never leave thee, nor forsake thee." Thus, on His own authority, Jesus assures us that we will never endure the desolation he experienced as he died in our place.

FORSAKEN

We have now come to one of the most haunting words of human life and experience. Such a dread word recalls for many an ocean of tears, heartache, bitter disappointment, destroyed faith, blighted hopes, and sorrowful loneliness. Jesus could bear being deserted by His chosen apostles, by the fickle popular crowd, and by the religious hierarchy, but desolation of soul caused by the hiding of His Father's face mystified Him. "Why hast thou forsaken me?" The extreme physical pain of crucifixion he endured did not baffle His mind, but the spiritual anguish of alienation from God did. The mystery of His broken heart is wrapped up in His cry, "Forsaken!" Spurgeon, preaching on the desolation Jesus endured, declared, "We can bear a bleeding body, and even a wounded spirit; but a soul conscious of desertion by God is beyond conception unendurable. When He holdeth back the face of His throne, and spreadeth His cloud upon it, who can endure the darkness?"

Although we have Martin Luther's expressive sentence on this Fourth Word, "God forsaken of God," the question as to whether Jesus was actually forsaken by His Father has been broached by several writers. Dealing with His mournful cry as being the genuine expression of the most perfect personal reality and truth, Krummacher asks, "Was Christ really forsaken of God while on the Cross? How could He be forsaken of God, Who was essentially one with Him, and when just at the moment of His unconditional obedient self-sacrifice on the Cross, He was the object of His supreme and paternal good pleasure?"

There are those scholars who seem to suggest that Jesus did not really mean what He said, that in His human weakness, He only *felt* that He was abandoned of God, just as many a distressed saint is sometimes tempted to believe when darkness seems to hide His face. I believe that Jesus said what He meant and meant what he said. While John the Baptist, alone in Herod's prison cell, had a period of depression and doubt as to whether Jesus was the promised Messiah, Jesus Himself did not doubt the reality of God, for twice He said, "My God, my God." What troubled His heart was the terrible and terrifying isolation He experienced during the three hours of dense darkness. He knew that He was never nearer and dearer to the heart of His Father in those hours because He was on the cross bearing the load of human iniquity God had placed upon His Son. James Stalker, whose monumental work, *The Trial and Death of Jesus,* is often referred to by writers dealing with the last hours of our Lord, says of the mystery of desertion:

> The deepest question of all is whether the desertion of Jesus was subjective or objective—that is, whether He had only, on account of bodily weakness and a temporary obscuration of the inward vision, a sense of being abandoned, or whether, in any real sense, God had actually forsaken Him.

Since "God was *in* Christ reconciling the world unto Himself," He could not be in the position of One forsaking His coequal in such reconciliation. The Father, Son, and Holy Spirit were three in *One,* unified in purpose as well as in deity. It was "through the eternal Spirit" that Jesus "offered Himself without spot to God," and if the Comforter was at the cross enabling Jesus to die, surely, the First Person of the Trinity was likewise present in supporting grace. The prophet says of God, "Thou art of purer eyes than to behold evil, and canst not look on iniquity" (Hab. 1:13).

The face of God, then, was not turned away from His wellbeloved Son but from what He was bearing, namely, the load of humanity's evil and iniquity. Believing that He was destined for "this hour" (John 12:27), was there "a momentary interruption of the conscious union between His human soul and the light of His Father's countenance, and feeling for one moment of the sense of abandonment which is the last weapon of the Enemy?" We must distinguish between the loss of God's presence and *a sense* of such a loss.

The terrible cry wrung from the soul of Jesus does express the hiding of the *consciousness* of the Father's presence, but not the absence of that august presence. Saints of old cried, "Why hidest thy face?" (Job 13:24; Ps. 44:24; 88:14; 104:28), but the face was still towards them, although hid. If through their sorrow and trials, they were bereft of the consciousness of God's nearness, He, nevertheless, was in their midst as He promised to be (Ps. 46). Canon Peter Green, dealing with the question about the Father separating Himself from His Son, with whom He was one, observes:

> If God turned away His face from the universe for one instant it would cease to exist. If He had turned His face away from Jesus, His human nature—the new humanity He brought into the world, and which on the Cross He was strengthening for you and me by victorious resistance to temptation—would have ceased to exist. It was the *sense* of His Father's presence that was withdrawn from Jesus during those dread hours of darkness.

From the inward consciousness of Jesus there was the feeling that God had withdrawn Himself, but the repetition, "My God, my God," proves that His naked faith struggled through all the pain and anguish of sin-bearing and assured Him that God was still His God and still with Him. There was the inward reverence of One in the presence of eternal majesty, and therefore, the confession, "Between thee and me there can never be any separation!" There was no failure of faith on the part of Jesus which led Him to imagine what was not an actual fact. The consciousness of a deserted Presence was the lowest depth of His grief in dying as the Savior of a lost world. God's comfortable fellowship had been withdrawn, and Jesus shivered under such a terrible deprivation. But there was no sign of faintness of heart or doubt toward the living God, as the mighty double grip of His unhesitating faith proves.

The question of paramount importance we must explore is the reason for the Lord's grief of mind over the absence of God's presence in such an hour of need. Why did God seem to desert His Son? What transpired during those three hours of unnatural, mysterious darkness which forced the cry of desolation from the lips of Jesus? Emerging from this period of intense gloom Jesus said, "It is finished"—or "accomplished," as the RV puts it, implying that throughout those hours of desertion a task of momentous significance was transacted. Before His crucifixion, Jesus, referring to it, declared, "For this cause came I unto this hour," and that such a cause would glorify his father (John 12:27–28). What was this preeminent cause? Was it not redemption for a world of sinners lost and ruined by the Fall? Spurgeon says, "The one Mediator between God and man, the Man Christ Jesus, beheld the holiness of God in arms against the sin of man, whose nature He had espoused. God was for Him and with Him in a certain unquestionable sense; but for the time, so far as His feeling went, God was against Him and necessarily withdrawn from Him."

Paul reminds us that we have been reconciled "in the body of His flesh through death" (Col. 1:21–22). Let us note the phrase "in the body of His flesh" because the great work of reconciliation was accomplished *in* the body of His flesh before He died physically. It is true that in various ways Paul describes how Jesus died for our sins according to the Scriptures, but the death that saves us from sin is the judicial death He died—the death He tasted for every man, as He drank the dreaded cup of God-forsakenness during those three hours of bitterest agony. As Dr. G. Campbell Morgan expressed it in his study on the cross:

> Redemption was not by the physical death of our Lord and Saviour, but something deeper and profounder than was accomplished and completed. The physical death was sacramental symbol wrought into visibility too profound for the fathoming of any philosophy or the interpretation of any theology.

During the hours preceding our Lord's paean of victory, Bengel says that "He suffered from the hand of God something unspeakable." It was in the "forsaking" that Jesus was bruised, put to grief, smitten, and afflicted by God for our iniquities. "The chastisement of our peace was upon Him" as He partook of the cup of desolation (Isa. 53:4–10). He had asked, "The cup which my Father hath given me, shall I not drink it?" (John 18:11). The cup was drained to its dregs, and having drunk, Jesus again asked the *why* of it. But with the "forsaking" past, communion with the Father was restored and Jesus triumphantly proclaims that the cause of such God-forsaken hours was past—the sin of the world—had been once and for all dealt with. The proclamation, "It is finished," indicated the completion of the act of our redemption.

With this Fourth Word we pass from Christ's outer circle of sorrow to his sufferings within, even to the abysmal evil of the burden of sin He was bearing for us. Often in the silence of the darkness of night He found consolation in communion with the Father, but now darkness becomes His enemy as He gave Himself to conquer the power of sin and death dragging man down to eternal woe. Yet because the plan of our redemption was conceived by God, His heart felt death in the dying heart of His beloved Son, who, as the Son of Man is the center of humanity requiring His salvation. As He tasted the sinfulness of sin and the bitterness of death for *every* man, none are beyond His ability to emancipate from sin's thraldom. While God was always infinitely well pleased with His beloved Son, yet as He gave Himself for others, He experienced the reverse side of the divine nature—the lightning of the divine wrath which struck Him. The vicarious endurance of this wrath, which was the penalty of the sins of the human race, was the cup the Father gave Him, and willingly He drank it.

While we cannot understand the mystery of all Jesus accomplished during those three hours when He felt exiled from the fellowship of God, we do believe the fact as expressed by Krummacher that, "Not only did all the horrors which were produced in the world from the dreadful womb of sin expand themselves before Him, but He also entered, with His holy soul, in a manner incomprehensible to us, into the fellowship of our consciousness of guilt and emptied the whole of the horrible cup of sin, of the wages of sin—that is, of the death involved in the curse, which was threatened in paradise." By the time the poignant cry *Eli, Eli, lama sabachthani?* was wrung from His agitated, broken heart, the battle had been won and Satan conquered. The justice of God had been satisfied and vindicated. Judicial wrath from the sword of the righteous Lord was endured when Jesus made His soul an offering for sin. Divine justice is inviolable.

During the desolate period when Jesus was bearing "the sins of many," His sinless soul was brought into contact with the sins of a lost world and the awful load crushed Him. In some mysterious way, "He was made sin for us" (Isa. 53:6; 2 Cor. 5:21; 1 Pet. 2:24): Sin in all its hideousness took possession of His human soul, and He underwent the full consciousness of God's wrath upon sin, enduring for a season the sense of that utter removal and banishment from God which is the supreme penalty and result of sin. If hell is, in part, eternal separation from God, then Jesus certainly had a foretaste of such bitterness when the sin of the world descended on Him in the place where judgment fell.

"Calvary was an awful revelation of the human heart," says Stalker, "whose enmity was directed straight against the perfect revelation of the love of God in Christ. There the sin of man reached its climax and did its worst. What was done there against Christ and against God in Him was a kind of embodiment and quintessence of the sin of the whole world. And, undoubtedly, it was this which was pressing on Jesus; this was the travail of His soul. He was looking close at sin's utmost hideousness; He was sickened with its contact; He was crushed with its brutality—crushed to death. . . . As the flower, by being crushed, yields up its fragrant essence, so He, by taking into His heart the sin of the world, brought salvation to the world."

As the Lamb of God, Jesus was provided to expiate and remove sin, to know divine government and justice, and to reconcile us to God. Dying, He presented to God an infinite atonement, and now we have redemption through His blood, even the forgiveness of our sins. He endured forsakenness that we might be forgiven. He paid our price, when He took our punishment and desolation and made them His own.

Utter loneliness was His that He might promise His redeemed ones, "I am with you always, even unto the end of the world." How can any sinner, who neglects and rejects such a great salvation, expect to escape eternal condemnation? Paul makes it clear that the impenitent are to be punished with everlasting destruction from the face of the Lord (2 Thess. 1:9, RV). In his most enlightening volume, *The Meaning of the Cross,* the great Methodist theologian, Dr. W. Russell Maltby, has this most forceful sentence:

> If to bear sins means to go where the sinner is, and refuse either to leave him or to compromise with him; to love a shameful being, and therefore to be pierced by his shame; to devote oneself utterly to his recovery, and to follow him with ceaseless ministries, knowing that he cannot be recovered without his consent, and that his consent may be definitely withheld—if this is to bear sin, then this is what Jesus did upon the Cross, and it is the innermost secret of the heart of God.

ME

This further pronoun was surely uttered with emphasis, "Why hast thou forsaken *me?*"—*me* above all others! I am the One you called your beloved Son in whom you were well pleased, and also the One who prayed, "Father, I know you always hear me." Did I not confess before others that you and I were one? Friend and foe have testified to my perfect innocence, that no guilt was found in my mouth, that there was no defect in my character, that I had never sinned or come short of thy glory or transgressed any commandment of thine. Why, then, didst *thou* forsake me—your only begotten Son?

The night of Christ's soul, however, was, that although He was holy, harmless, undefiled, separate from sinners, having God's nearness His paradise and God's love His bliss, yet it was such a One who, for our sakes, was forsaken of God at the moment of His unconditional obedient self-sacrifice for our sins on the cross. Thus, behind His *me* we can read His thought, "Why leave me desolate, and am I not still thy child in whom thou hast delight? Why wilt thou not

cause thy face to shine upon me, and be gracious unto me?"
Through grace we know that His mournful cry on the cross,
although altogether inexplicable, meant our eternal redemption; that "death and the curse were in His cup," that
ours might be the cup of salvation. After His cry, the darkness was dispelled and the sun was restored to its full midday splendor, symbolic of the transformation that takes place
when a sinner, reconciled to God through the redemption
of the cross, passes from darkness into His marvelous light.

Precious are the lessons, then, stored up in our hearts
against the future. The first is that God's afflictive dealings
with us are prompted by a Father's love, who delights to
trust His trustworthy children with trials bringing glory to
His name and permanent enlargement of heart and blessing
for themselves, and through them, for others. Periods of
darkness may overtake us but from the dark night the Lord
passed through light ever arises. We have the promise that
no one or nothing can ever separate us from the love of
God in Christ, who was forsaken that the righteous need
never know what it is to be forsaken. As Spurgeon expresses
it:

> As to my sin, I hear its harsh accusings no more when I hear
> Jesus say, "Why hast thou forsaken me?" I know that I deserve
> the deepest hell at the hand of God's vengeance; but I am not
> afraid, He will never forsake *me*, for He forsook His Son on
> my behalf.

How strengthened we are as we face the inexplicable trials
of life and contemplate Him who knew the agony of pain
and suffered darkness and death that He might turn death
into life and darkness into light for all those redeemed by
His precious blood! In desolate hours we may rejoice that
He knows our path, and that in our sickness and sorrow He
cares for us. If the Lord should permit a furnace of affliction,
like the three Hebrew youths of old, we, too, can have the
assurance of the presence of Him whose form is like that of
the Son of God. With the confidence of faith we can say,
"Thou wilt not, canst not, and darest not forsake me, O God,

because the merits of thy only-begotten Son forever bind thee to me." When days of darkness seem to veil His face we can triumphantly sing

> There may be days of darkness and distress,
> When sin has power to tempt, and care to press,
> Yet in the darkest day I will not fear,
> For, 'mid the shadows, Thou wilt still be near.

The Fifth Word of Love

LOVE THAT SUFFERS

"Jesus said, I thirst"
John 19:28

Love That Suffers

Paul would have us know that "love suffereth long," or is long-suffering, or, as we can put it—"long on suffering." Evidence can be found in many homes of the amazing ability of true love to suffer and to be kind. Such love is strong as death. The Bible clearly proves that divine love is a love that not only suffers but is long on suffering. When rejected by those it suffers for, it burns with a more intense flame. Bishop Wordsworth has taught us to sing:

> Love is kind, and suffers long;
> Love is meek, and thinks no wrong;
> Love than death itself more strong:
> Therefore give us Love.

Calvary is the supreme example of how love can suffer. It was because of His supreme love for sinners that Jesus endured the cross and despised its shame. When He said, "I thirst," He opened a window on all the pain and agony of dying such a death as crucifixion. It wasn't roman nails that kept Him fastened to the cross but an undying love for

101

a world that rejected Him. Jesus' Fourth Word from the cross reveals "the climax of the struggle which had gone on in the mind of the Divine Sufferer during the three hours of silence and darkness which preceded its utterance and as the liberation of His mind from that struggle."

Bishop Wilson, in his meditation on, *The Patience of Christ,* reminds us of the capacity of Jesus to suffer:

> What sorrows did He undergo, and with what patience did He suffer them! Patient when Judas unworthily betrayed Him with a kiss; patient when Caiaphas despitefully used Him; patient when hurried from one place to another; patient when Herod with his men of war set Him at nought; patient when Pilate so unrighteously condemned Him; patient when scourged and crowned with thorns; patient when His Cross was laid upon Him; patient when He was reviled, reproached, scoffed at, and in every way abused. Lord Jesus grant me loving patience after this example, to bear Thy Holy will in all things.

THE SHORTEST OF THE SAYINGS

While John records the cry in two words, "I thirst," in the language in which Jesus spoke the statement is a single word. It is the shortest of the Seven Words and can be compared with another short verse John gives, "Jesus wept" (John 11:35). David James Burrell says of this one word cry that "it is as brief and simple as the wail of a little child. The chronicler makes no comment, attempts no explanation. This is characteristic of the Holy Scriptures." If there had been the sensational journals and papers we now have, what a harrowing delineation of Christ's death they would have given: "His blanching face, the fever-bursting eyes, the parched lips!" But there is nothing of this in the sacred narrative: "After this Jesus saith, I thirst."

Although this utterance is only one brief bare word in the Greek, no other could rival the simplicity and suffering it conveys. Of this shortest of all the words uttered on Calvary, Spurgeon has this apt comment, "I cannot say that it is short and sweet, for, alas, it was bitterness itself to our Lord Jesus; and yet out of its bitterness I trust there will come great sweetness to us. Though bitter to Him in the speaking, it will be sweet to us in the hearing—so sweet that all the bitterness of our trials shall be forgotten as we remember the vinegar and gall of which He drank."

THE FIRST REFERENCE TO PERSONAL SUFFERING

Up to this moment no word of his own need had escaped the lips of Jesus. His thoughts had been of others—for those standing by and for all the people of the world. As our meditation on the previous Words prove, it was not until all else had been accomplished—His murderers forgiven, a penitent sinner welcomed home to paradise, His loved ones provided for, and the enemy met and conquered that the Son of man thought of the agony racking His tortured body. It was not until the completion of His sacrificial work, as prophesied of old, that He became conscious of His human need and cried, "I thirst." Mental agony was past—now bodily suffering is felt.

Thus, among the last words of Jesus on the cross His physical pain claims only one word, *dipsaō*. From His parched lips there drops this expressive word, summing up in itself all His body had lovingly endured on our behalf. The previous cry was one describing His soul in desolation, this one, for something to slake His now conscious thirst, came from the body in its extreme weakness. Such a statement, "I thirst," or "I am thirsty," must have been a relief to Jesus to utter, for the worst pain He endured on the cross was not that of the body but of the soul, when mystified by the hiding of God's face. The tide of that anguish has passed now, and there comes a solitary word expressing a human need. Now that the darkness is past with its absorption in the gigantic struggle against the forces of evil and our deliverance from satan and hell is secured, Jesus realizes His physical state. "I thirst," was a significant signal to the cry of spiritual desolation, "Why hast thou forsaken me?"

It is worthy of notice that in this Fifth Word Jesus did not ask for liquid to quench His burning thirst but simply stated the fact of His physical need, "I am thirsty." Stalker reminds us that "intense mental occupation has a tendency to cause the oblivion of bodily wants," and goes on to relate a conversation he had with a German soldier severely wounded in the Franco-Prussian War whose one agony swallowed up all the rest of his suffering and made him forget his wounds and peril. It was the agony of thirst, and the helpless soldier would have given anything for a drink of water. Manifested to destroy the works of the devil, it was essential for our Lord to be tempted by him in all points like as we are, and so at the outset of His public ministry there came the grim encounter with the devil. Forty days and forty nights the conflict raged during which period Jesus fasted. He was oblivious to bodily needs, but as soon as the temptation was past we read that "He hungered."

The same experience was His on the cross when "through death He might destroy him that had the power of death, that is, the devil." While the agonies of the horrible death by crucifixion were of "the most excruciating and complicated order," Jesus endured them, as He did the three hours of intense darkness, but after a time "they all gathered into one central current in which they were lost and swallowed up—that of devouring thirst, and it was this that drew from our Lord the Fifth Word." But although *dipsaō* was His only cry of physical pain after being absorbed either in caring for others or in prayer to God, He did utter this one cry which proved Him to be One made like unto us.

Jesus will ever be recognized by the honest, helpful confession, "I thirst," as the One who shared our life of instinct, desire, and sensitive nerves—the One who entered wholly into the fellowship of humanity and was not free from pain. It is this, as Dryden puts it, that is "the porcelain clay of human kind." Jesus was no "pale Galilean," but one Who had the normal instincts of man and knew how to suffer. When a loved one is dying, close by stands a dear one ministering to the last desire, wetting the fevered lips. The bitter cry of Jesus discovers His full identification with us for, in anguish, at the last moment He said, "I am thirsty."

A further lesson to be gleaned from Jesus' one and only word of agony is that His denial of self and thoughtfulness for others left Him little time to dwell upon His own pain and anguish. One Word out of seven calling attention to His torture is a call to us not to dwell too much on His merely physical sufferings on the cross but rather upon all that He accomplished for our salvation as He endured the cross. We should meditate more upon His mental and spiritual sufferings than upon His bodily anguish; more upon His sacrificial love than upon the blood that flowed from His wounds. While the New Testament epistles have much to say about "the precious blood," it is the surrendered life for our redemption the blood symbolizes that the writers extol.

All who suffer greatly in body are grateful for the single word Jesus pleadingly uttered, for it sanctifies their pain to remember "what pains He had to bear." It must be remembered however, that He didn't bear all the physical anguish the cross entailed simply to show us how to suffer nobly and resignedly, but rather that we might be emancipated from the guilt and power of sin.

THE DOUBLE DRAUGHT

Archbishop William Alexander suggests that there are three draughts connected with the Cross: "The *first* is the proffered opiate, refused because He meets death without respite or alleviation. The *second* is the mock wassil-cup, the caricature of the imperial coronation wine. The *third* is that of the draught He resistlessly needed (Matt. 27:34; Luke 23:36; John 19:29) ."

The second draught was a bowl of vinegar or wine free from the myrrh or gall the Roman soldiers had brought to refresh themselves with as they remained on guard beside the crosses. Luke reminds us that it was this innocent beverage the soldiers put to a callous use when the thirst of Jesus was held up for grievous insult: "And the soldiers also mocked Him, coming to Him, and offering Him vinegar, and saying, If thou be the king of the Jews, save thyself" (23:36–37) .

What I want to emphasize here are the two drinks Jesus was offered—one at the beginning of his Passion, as mentioned by Matthew, and the other at the end of the Passion, offered by compassionate soldiers. The first drink He refused, the second He requested when He cried, "I am thirsty." As Hoffman expresses it, "Jesus refused the intoxicating draught, before the crucifixion began, that His senses might be kept clear; and that now He accepted the refreshing draught for the same purpose."

THE FIRST DRINK

Matthew's explicit statement is, "They gave him vinegar to drink mingled with gall: and when he had tasted thereof, he would not drink" (27:34). Why did He definitely refuse to take this proffered draught? Because as soon as He tasted it, He knew its nature and purpose. This was a cup Jesus would not drink seeing it was a stupefying concoction given to those prepared for crucifixion to deaden their sense of pain. Mark says that the drink was wine mingled with gall (15:23), while Matthew describes it as vinegar tinctured with gall. The drink, in which myrrh and gall are treated as being synonymous, is prophetically referred to in Psalm 69:21. Vinegar, the thin sour wine of the people, and the myrrh corresponds to the gall, both of which possessed narcotic properties. It was a kind of ancient form of chloroform and was provided in a humane spirit by those who wanted to help condemned malefactors become oblivious to the terrible sufferings and fate before them. As Dr. W. R. Matthews states in his study on *The Two Thirsts:*

> Even in those brutal days, when men's hearts were, it seems like the nether stone for hardness, there were some who had the imagination and sympathy to wish to lessen the torture of criminals; just as in those other days, not less cruel, when Christians burnt each other for the glory of God, there were often compassionate men who mixed gunpowder with the faggots, so that the suffering of the heretic might be shortened.

Doubtless the two thieves, crucified with our Lord, were offered the natural sedative and gratefully accepted the sour draught to make them insensible to pain, and who, consequently, would not suffer the pang of thirst so long as the effect of the drug remained. But when the merciful stupefying drink was offered Jesus, who must have appreciated such an act of kindness, tasting the wine and smelling the myrrh, He refused the provided anodyne. Why? The only answer is that He declined to be released from the experience of the crucifixion by any invention or interference of man. Having set His face steadfastly toward the cross, He must not challenge the last enemy of men whom He had come to redeem with blunted will or senses stupefied.

Jesus determined to permit nothing that would cloud His soul as He tasted death for every man. All the physical and mental agony of the cross was part of the ingredient of the other cup He had received from His Father's hand in Gethsemane, and thus He would avoid nothing in that cup of sorrow. For the security of a perfect salvation for a sinning race, it was of cardinal importance that consciousness, self-possession, and poise should be the Savior's. And, "it was to this high resolve to keep His faculties unclouded that we owe the Seven Last Words." How grateful we should be for His refusal of the first drink! Had He been drugged and made insensible to pain and feeling as He hung upon the cross, He would not have been the Savior we need. But because He endured those hours of unrelieved suffering and faced the terrors of pain and death, conscious every moment of His anguish, He is our friend and guide wherever our path may lead.

Hubert Simpson relates the incident of a professor in a British university "who refused to allow his physical suffering to be relieved with morphia, in order that with undulled sense he might finish the dictating of his book which was the creed that had become his by right of conquest, to which he gave the fine title of *A Faith That Enquires*. His last words were an ascription of praise and thanksgiving to Almighty God."

> All fiery pangs on battlefields,
>   On fever beds where sick men toss,
> Are in that human cry He yields
>   To anguish on the Cross.

THE LAST DRINK

The further draught offered Jesus in response to His moan, "I thirst" was gratefully accepted when an unknown warrior ran to succor Jesus with undrugged wine, the sour beverage which was a Roman soldier's daily ration. Matthew reminds us that it was only after the devil had left Jesus that "angels came and ministered unto him" (4:11). At Calvary, after the accomplishment of His God-given task of redemption, He cried, "I thirst," and gratefully accepts the offered refreshment. This Fifth Word was not a request, as when Jesus said to the woman at the well, "Give me to drink." On the cross He did not appeal for relief, but instinctively uttered a spontaneous cry of intense suffering. And, as Archbishop Marcus Loane asks:

> Who can refuse a cup of cold water? Who can ignore the thirst of the dying? Hagar cried out for thirst, and an angel led her to an unseen well, Genesis 21:19. Israel cried out for thirst, and waters gushed out from the smitten rock, Exodus 17:6. The God Who heard their cry of thirst would not allow this cry to pass without a prompt reply.

This last earthly solace of Jesus was not water but "a vessel full of vinegar." It was the undiluted, undrugged wine the soldiers used to assuage their own thirst. As the cross was in its upright position it was not easy to reach the Sufferer's lips, so the thoughtful soldier took a sponge and emptied his bottle of wine—perhaps the wine he was drinking at his midday meal—and then fixed the sponge on the end of a long, stiff reed of a hyssop plant and pressed it against the dry lips of Jesus for Him to moisten them and suck the sponge dry. Marcus Loane points out that the verb Matthew uses for this incident implies that he kept on pressing the sponge to the Savior's lips until He felt relieved of thirst. How He must have welcomed and gratefully accepted this strengthening draught! Now Jesus is able to continue keeping His senses clear as the end of His travail draws near. Now He can lay down His life for others with every faculty alive and with every sense engaged. He had declared that

He had power to lay down His life and that no man could take it from Him by making Him dazed and half stupefied by a drug. Having, through His once offering of Himself as a sacrifice to banish sin, Jesus drank the draught the sympathetic soldier had offered Him.

THE UNKNOWN SOLDIER

Among the conspicuous vaults in Westminster Abbey, London, is that oft-visited one bearing the inscription "To the Unknown Soldier." Chosen from among the thousands who died in battle during World War I, his buried remains in the nation's famous shrine serves to remind all who stand at his grave of the sacrifice of the millions who died. Would it not be most interesting to know the name of the unknown soldier who was kind to Jesus as he made a supreme sacrifice for our salvation? The Gospels, however, preserve his anonymity, just as they do with the woman who slaked the thirst of Jesus at Sychar's Well.

The soldier, whose heart was touched by the need of Jesus, was one hardened to deeds of cruelty in long Roman campaigns, yet he disregarded his comrades when they mocked him saying, "Now let us see whether Elias will come to save him," after heeding the dying Savior's mortal cry, "I thirst." The drink he offered Jesus will be remembered as a memorial to his kindness forever. As a group, the soldiers at the cross despised the crucified Galilean, but the one who pressed the cooling sponge to the parched lips of Jesus was moved to pity. Yet if John's language is literally pressed, "*They* filled a sponge with vinegar," more than one of the company took part in that act of pity. "Strange are the ways of Providence!" says Hubert Simpson. "As once by the well of Sychar it was given to a loose woman to quench His thirst, so now, at the well of the world's salvation, a rough soldier ministers to His need. First a Samaritan, and now a Roman. He belonged to the whole world." The soldier without a name, but not without compassion, may have been a pagan, but he stands out in the carnival of hate at the cross as one who showed mercy. Although this man was among the executioners, Jesus accepted from him the drink he offered. In fact, this soldier was the only one in the crowd around the cross to think of Jesus in His need, and his was the one solitary act of kindness shown to Jesus in His agony.

Matthew gave us a most captivating feature of this helper of Jesus when he wrote that the soldier *"ran . . . and gave him to drink,"* so eager was he to relieve the Savior's thirst. Quite a contrast from the different attitude of those who "stood afar off, beholding that sight." It is hard for us to imagine a rough, tough Roman soldier running to succor a helpless victim, especially the One who but lately had been the butt of his and his comrades' coarse jests. Are we among the few who are prompt to run with the sponge? Do we serve the Lord with alacrity in His thirst for the salvation of souls? What prompted this nameless soldier to respond so speedily to the cry of thirst? We are not told. Probably he was ashamed of his former conduct and sought forgiveness by his act of kindness, or he may have been impelled by a sense of human compassion. For all we know, the Crucified Himself may have laid it on the heart of this heathen fighter to relieve His thirst.

According to tradition, the work of grace began to work in the unregenerate heart of this soldier and he became a Christian. James Stalker reminds us that "all His life Jesus had been wont to discover more good in the worst than others believed to exist, and to the last He remained true to His own faith. . . . He believed there were some drops of the milk of human kindness even in the hardhearted Roman soldiers; and He was not disappointed. But no one could have relieved Jesus as the young soldier did and remained hardened and unbelieving, and so the story is that the plight and attitude of Jesus as He died resulted in the conversion of this man who 'gave Him to drink,' just as His request to the Samaritan woman led to her conversion. Does not Matthew tell us that the soldiers as well as the centurion 'were with him, watching Jesus . . . feared greatly, saying, 'Truly this was the Son of God?' " (27:54).

That Roman soldier has left us a good example to emulate. We might well envy him the opportunity of satisfying our Lord's bodily thirst and of accomplishing the one act of kindness He received while dying as our substitute. Yet to each of us comes the privilege of showing in most practical ways our love and gratitude for our Lord's sacrificial love. All kindness, pity, and sympathy shown to the sinful and needy in some way lessens the pain of Calvary. The soldier gave liberally of what he had to alleviate the suffering of Jesus, and His cry is still heard through the world, "I thirst." In serving others, we serve Him, for did He not say, "Inasmuch as ye did it unto the least of these my brethren, ye did it unto me"? Little did that nameless helper know how vital and good was the act he performed, and that by it he assisted in rolling away the cloud that had enveloped the soul of Jesus. For three hours Jesus was caught up in the toils of suffering and sin as He effected our reconciliation with God, but refreshed by the draught, He looked up into the face of the Father—the sense of whose presence He had lost awhile—and saw satisfaction and peace. He saw something sure and steadfast, enabling Him to entrust the safe keeping of His soul to God and die in triumph saying, "Father, into thy hands I commend my spirit." In like manner, we will never know what consecrated service on our part means to Him, and to those He enables us to assist. Marcus Loane says:

> Who would not wish that he might have been there to cool His lips and quench His thirst? Yet the thirst of His lips was as nothing to the thirst of His soul, for the Son of Man was athirst for God, and for the souls of men. The great longing of His heart for human love and trust still throbs through that cry; this was the pain of heart which can never grow less while there are sheep outside the fold for whom He died. Thus we may still hear the far-off echo of that cry from the Cross: *I thirst!* We may also hear how He asks of us as He once asked of old *Give Me to drink*. And to those who truly refresh His heart, assuage His thirst, and bring Him joy, He will yet have this word to say, *"I was thirsty, and ye gave Me drink."*

There is a further aspect about the two drinks offered Jesus we can apply to ourselves as suggested by Hubert Simpson in the phrase, "Our Lord, as ever holding the mean between indulgence of the flesh and fanatical refusal of the merciful provisions of God, drank what the thoughtful ranker offered Him." Jesus refused the "vinegar mingled with gall," seeing he was adverse to any avenue of escape from the agony of the cross. If we are among those redeemed by His blood and know that we have been saved to serve, we can expect to be offered satanic stupefying draughts designed to make us insensible to sacrifice anything for Him who, with unclouded mind, endured His cross. Easier and painless ways of Christian living and serving may be accepted because of the immediate satisfaction they give, but these are not the way of Calvary, which is the only way to live passionately or fully. "All the anguish of disappointment which comes to every spirit striving for good in the midst of evil will pass by our deadened souls and leave them untouched. . . . Those who plumb the depths of passion and see the adventure out are they who, like Jesus, will remain fully conscious to the end, dissipating no fraction of the power within them, but concentrating it upon the Kingdom of God, satisfied with nothing less than the new wine of the Kingdom."

Another error to guard ourselves against, founded upon Christ's refusal of the narcotic wine to deaden pain, is that of the refusal of anesthetics and drugs which science has developed for the alleviation of pain. The argument of religious people who act thus is that the acceptance of such means of physical relief is an interference with God's providential government. Members of the Jehovah's Witnesses cult are prepared to see one of their number die rather than allow a blood transfusion that will continue life. Christian Science also denies the actual existence of sickness and suffering, and has its "Mind-Healers." Jesus, however, differs from us in that He came to die for our sins and in the sounding of the depths of human woe and tasting death for all men, it was imperative for Him not to be drugged and therefore unable to know what He was dying for.

OUR LORD'S DUAL NATURE

The pronoun and noun forming the cry, "I thirst," also suggests a striking witness of the combination of our Lord's deity and humanity. "I," as used by Jesus, reveals Him as the Son of God. When He affirmed, "My Father and I are one," He implied that He was co-equal with the Father. Emphasis is first of all then on the "I," with all the authority and power the pronoun implies when used by Jesus. "I am thirsty." The great I AM thirsty! It seems incredible. As co-Creator of heaven and earth, He brought into being the oceans, seas, and rivers. He is "The Fountain of Living Waters," and the One who, in the last day, the great day of the feast, stood and cried, "If any man thirst, let him come unto me and drink"—yet here from the cross He appeals, "I thirst."

At Cana of Galilee, in order to add to the pleasure for the guests at a wedding, Jesus turned water into wine—and the best wine at that. And a little later Jesus said to the Samaritan woman that whoever drank of the living water He was able to give would never thirst again. Yet, startlingly omnipotent in supplying the needs of others, He finds Himself smitten with thirst. Throughout His brief ministry of just over three years we have this striking contrast between His deity and His destitution. He could affirm, "*I am* the bread of life," but yet knew what it was to be hungry for a meal. He could say, "The silver and the gold are mine," yet He allowed Himself to be supported by the women who ministered unto Him of their substance. Before He went out to His cross, Jesus promised His disciples thrones and many mansions, yet He confessed that He had nowhere to lay His head. Although made in "the form of God" and deeming it no "robbery to be equal with God," there came the hiding of His power as, for instance, in His refusal to perform a miracle and provide the refreshment He needed in His agony. When He cried, "I thirst," He refused to present an outward and visible manifestation of His Godhead and allowed a nameless soldier to meet His need. As Bishop Lightfoot expressed it, "He emptied, stripped Himself of the insignia of Majesty."

If the "I" expresses the essential deity of Jesus, then the verb "thirst" reveals His absolute humanity. If, in the "I" we see Him as the Son of God, in the "thirst" we behold Him as the Son of Man—bone of our bone and flesh of our flesh, and as such He was tried or tested like as we are, yet without sin. His appeal, "I thirst," has been called "the cry of the human." It may seem strange to us that Jesus should speak of thirst as He was about to die and go to His Father. Although His physical agony was extreme, and a few moments longer could not have mattered much, yet we have His appeal "I thirst," signifying how intense His pain must have been.

Pangs of thirst are among the most terrible sufferings man can endure. Hunger can numb his vital powers, but thirst will not allow its victim one moment of insensibility. And the Son of God who became the Son of Man experienced the agony of such thirst and was relieved when a hardened executioner yielded to the dictates of compassion. Because of His manhood, His bodily pain was real, and the soldier who gave Jesus wine to drink recognized His humanity and His helplessness. The Lord of Glory, then, in asking for a drink, revealed how real His humanity was. Being severely wounded and exhausted even before He reached the cross, and then, the dread hours stretched upon it, must have produced an insatiable thirst, but He endured it for our sakes. His simple cry of human need, "I am thirsty," proved his sympathy with every form of physical, mental, and spiritual perplexity and distress. He was not above confessing His human weakness and weariness in His one and only indication of physical suffering. "It was Jesus alone Who cried aloud in the extremity of need, for that cry of thirst was part of His self-sacrifice for man."

Spurgeon calls the cry "I thirst," *the ensign of His humanity.* The Psalmist reminds us that, "The mighty God, even the Lord, hath spoken. . . . If I were hungry, I would not tell thee" (Ps. 50). But when God the Son, became the Man of Sorrows and had need of drink, He voiced His need for men to hear and received it from one whose heart was stirred by His appeal. As to the reality of His sufferings, there can be no doubt, just as it is clearly evident that all the anguish the cross represents was borne in the perfection of His human nature. All the sorrows of man were carried by the Man of Sorrows. Is not His call, "Behold and see if there be any sorrow like unto my sorrow"? He had power to prevent His agony for, by a miracle, He could have destroyed the whole Roman army and freed Himself, but He wove a stern necessity into His cross. "The Son of Man *must* be lifted up." Jesus willingly entered into a region of shame, mystery, sorrow, and pain for our sin, and it is only by His stripes that we can be healed.

THE PROPHETIC TABLEAU

In recording the thirst of Jesus, John reminds us of the connection of Old Testament Scripture with the events in the life of Jesus who could say of so many ancient truths, "These are they that testify of me." After His resurrection from the dead Jesus could say, "These are the words which I spake unto you, while I was yet with you, that all things must be fulfilled, which were written in the law of Moses, and in the prophets, and in the psalms, concerning me" (Luke 24:44). We know how the Psalms were deeply written into His own life. About one thousand years before the cross, it was written, "In my thirst they gave me vinegar to drink" (Ps. 69:22), and John has no hesitation in proclaiming this statement as a prophetic forecast of his Master's cry, "I thirst" and the response it secured. The Apostle introduces the Fifth Word by saying, "Jesus, knowing that all things were now accomplished, that the Scripture might be fulfilled, saith, I thirst."

When Jesus voiced the cry of thirst, it was not an effort to fulfill the Psalmist's particular prediction. Rather it was that Jesus had to endure this anguish of the cross because it had been foreordained and forecast for Him to do so. The soldiers cast lots for the seamless robe of Jesus "that the Scripture might be fulfilled." This cannot mean that the soldiers acted with a *deliberate purpose* of ensuring the accomplishment of Scripture, but with the *result* of its being fulfilled. Likewise, John's record proves that *"thirst* was part of the martyr-image of Messiah in the mirror of the Psalms." As the kind of death Jesus died was unknown in Old Testament times, being conceived as a form of capital punishment by the Romans who were not in existence in David's day, what he forecast so precisely of the crucifixion is one of the greatest proofs of divine inspiration (Ps. 22:18). Is this not why the Scriptures are a great comfort to our hearts? All He has promised to do for us, He will perform (Matt. 24:35).

THE UNDYING THIRST

When Jesus rose from the dead, He resumed all Godhead activities, and when He ascended on high, it was in a glorified body—a body the apostles could see and which He Himself declared still bore the marks of the nails. But it was a body that required no food or drink for its sustenance. Natural hunger and thirst, such as Jesus experienced in the days of His flesh were instincts omitted from His risen body. Says John of the redeemed in Glory, "They shall hunger no more, neither thirst any more. . . . For the Lamb . . . shall feed them, and shall lead them unto living fountains of waters" (Rev. 7:16, 17). There is no contradiction here for what John is emphasizing is the passing of human instincts and the manifestation of spiritual instincts and desires. Physically, the Lord's thirst, such as He expressed, is over, but vicariously He still thirsts, for, according to His teaching, when we give a cup of water to a thirsty soul, we are giving Him to drink (Matt. 25:42–46).

Is the impulse of humanity as strong in us as it was in the soldier who gave Jesus what He desired? Throughout the Church His appeal rolls, "I thirst," and it is for us to hear Christ in His afflicted ones—in the countless thousands who die of actual thirst in a drought-ridden land like India—and to know that when we strive to relieve them, it is like "lifting the sponge to pass over those pale and dying lips." The world around is perishing for the lack of the water of life. Brothers and sisters of Jesus are sitting and suffering in lonely rooms wishing some kind friend would visit them or they may be lying on beds of pain and needing someone to come and ease their pillow or reach the cup to dry lips. Jesus is there saying, "Inasmuch as ye did it unto one of the least of these my brethren, ye did it unto me." It is insufficient to weep at Calvary as if our tears were the sole evidence of our devotion to Jesus.

The One who cried, "I thirst," tells us plainly how we can satisfy His thirst. Those who drink at earthly fountains only to thirst and stagger on in their deep need, must be led to Him who said, "Whosoever drinketh of the water that I shall give shall never thirst again." The hungry and naked, the sick and those in prison—Jesus said that their pain is His pain, and He depends on us to give them the satisfying draught. If we truly love Jesus, ours will be the undying effort to take Him out to the needy, whether they are afflicted spiritually, physically, or materially. He alone has the solace of life.

> There is a doorway in a narrow street,
> And close beside that door a broken stair,
> And then a low, dark room.
>   The room is bare;
> But in the corner lies
> A worn-out form upon a hard straw-bed,
> No pillow underneath his aching head;
> A face grown wan with suffering, and a hand
> Scarce strong enough to reach the small, dry crust
> That lies upon the chair.
> "Go in," the Master says, "for I am there!
> I have been waiting wearily in that cold room,
> Waiting long, lonely hours,
> Waiting for thee to come."

Although the thirst Jesus suffered on the cross was of a physical nature, yet His appeal, "I thirst" has spiritual connotations. Near His end, Jesus thirsted to reach His goal, namely, the entire fulfillment of Scripture—the completion of a God-given task—the full enjoyment of the light of His Father's face upon the consummation of our redemption. The thirst of His body was nothing compared with His spiritual thirst for His Father. In a higher and fuller sense than David, Jesus could say, "My soul thirsteth for God, for the living God. . . . My flesh longeth for thee in a dry and thirsty land, where no water is." Such a thirst had been His from the earliest of His earthly days. When only twelve years of age, He said, "Wist ye not that I must be about my Fa-

ther's business?" Do we share this thirst of the Master to have
God at the center and circumference of our daily life?

Thirsting for God implies thirsting after His righteousness, and for the fulfillment of scriptural precepts in our
lives. "Thirst," whether physical or spiritual, is an instinct.
"If thirst were not an instinct, the human race would be ex-
tinct—or rather, it could not have existed at all." As babes
thirst for all a mother can give, so our souls thirst for our
Maker and all He has for us. Anna L. Waring has taught us
to sing,

> Now the frail vessel Thou hast made,
> No hand but Thine shall fill;
> The waters of this world have failed,
> And I am thirsty still.

How blessed we are when, with the Psalmist, we, too, can
confess, "My soul thirsts for Thee like a parched land" (Ps.
143:6). John R. W. Stott tells us that, "The Christian is a
spiritual dipsomaniac, always thirsty, always drinking." Is
this our experience as those who believe the invitation of
Jesus, "If any man thirst, let him *come* to me and drink"?
The question is, We have the *invitation,* but are we diligent
in our appropriation of the draught he freely offers? As one
writer states it, "If *thirst* is Jesus' condition for our coming
to Him for power, then it follows that *drinking* will be the
means of appropriation." And the promise He gives us is that
if we stoop and drink the living water found in Him, we
shall never thirst again, or as the context implies, "Shall
never thirst *for anything else*" (John 4:14).

Another object of Jesus' undying thirst is that of thirst for
the souls of men—a thirst that brought Him down from the
ivory palaces to take upon Himself the garb of our humanity
and become the Son of Man in order to seek and save the
lost. He came into the world to receive and redeem sinners
and by His death and redemption provided a sinful and sinning world with a perfect salvation. As Lange, the well-
known commentator, expressed it:

Jesus thirsted to drink of the refreshment of love—for a final human greeting, for human blessing. And if we pursue this to its deepest meaning, we may say that He, with a special depth of feeling, thirsted for the souls of men.

Can we say that we share Jesus' travail for the souls of men? An early father of the Church said, "Jesus thirsted that we might thirst." What are we doing to spread the saving knowledge of Him who died for the salvation of the lost? He made peace by the blood of His cross, and by the time He cried, "Why didst thou forsake me?" the work of reconciliation and atonement was completed. When He came to cry "I thirst," He hinted at His intense desire to see multitudes participating in His finished work of redemption.

Jesus ever thirsts for the evangelization of people all over the world, irrespective of their nationality or color of skin, and He plainly tells us how we can help to satisfy His thirst, "Go ye into all the world and preach the gospel to every creature." Thirsty physically, He said to the woman at the well, "Give me to drink," and He would have us tell a lost world that He is the Savior, thirsting for the salvation of the lost. Through the lips of millions of sin-sick souls, Jesus speaks and calls us *today* to assist Him. He thirsts for them and calls us to labor with Him in leading them to Him who is the Fountain of living waters. Jesus thirsts for our acts of love and self-sacrifice in the assuaging of His thirst for souls. But are we experiencing the joy of holding the sponge to the lips of Jesus, and by His Spirit, assisting Him to see of the travail of His soul and be satisfied?

Thou sayest this sad day *I thirst* again,
And I, remembering how, to ease Thy pain,
Some harsh-faced Roman, stained and scarred with war,

Gave Thee his vinegar,
 (And earned a fuller comfort than he gave),
Go forth to seek for Thee at Thy behest
Not only such suave souls as please me best;
But rough sour souls that Thou did'st parch to save.

As the Head of His Church, Jesus is in Glory and thirsts on earth in His members, and will acknowledge from the throne of His glory their service when they see Him thirsty and give the world drink. Such blessed soul-thirst of true Christian love helps in the complete pattern of Christ crucified for the ungodly. He died for the souls of men and still has an intense thirst for humanity and a great passion for His kingdom for which we have the opportunity of laboring. All saints can serve the King in both material and spiritual things until His thirst will be fully satisfied when we see Him in His beauty.

But what of those who in spite of all divine and human entreaty will not "stoop down and drink and live"? Jesus once portrayed the terrible plight of one in the invisible world who rejected Jesus as the life-giving Stream. He was smitten by a thirst far worse than any bodily torment. The rich man in hell was agonized by a nameless inward thirst and called upon Lazarus, who was constantly hungry and thirsty on earth, to come to him in his dire need and dip the tip of his finger in water and cool his parched tongue. But in hell there is no refreshing draught—nothing but an unending thirst for the pure river of the water of life, clear as crystal, which flows only from the throne of the Lamb who was slain. Thus the rich man's request was refused without mercy, seeing he had finally spurned such water of life. Knocking at heaven's gates from the habitations of eternal night gained no response. Rejecting the Love that has suffered for his salvation, he found himself beyond the aid of such Love.

The Sixth Word of Love

LOVE THAT TRIUMPHS

"It is finished."
John 19:30

Love That Triumphs

Charles Wesley must have had heaven's triumphant Love in mind when he penned these words:

> Love, like death, hath all destroyed,
> Rendered all distinctions void;
> Names, and sects, and parties fall;
> Thou, O Christ, art all in all.

In His exclamation of achievement, "It is finished," Jesus sang His song of triumph, as quaint Edward Spenser of the fifteenth century indicated in one of his sonnets:

> Most glorious Lord of life, that on this day
> Didst make Thy triumph over death and sin:
> And having harrow'd Hell, didst bring away
> Captivity thence captive, us to win.

Among the graces, Paul gives the preeminence to love because of its victories as well as virtues: "Love never faileth." Thus, as Spenser continues in his sonnet:

123

So let us love, dear Love, like as we ought,
Love is the lesson which the Lord us taught.

The most stupendous triumph of love was achieved at Calvary, and was proclaimed by Him who died as the Son of the God who loved the world, particularly in His Sixth Word, "It is finished."

THE MOST MOMENTOUS WORD EVER UTTERED

It has been pointed out that in the course of history and in our own lives a single word has had far-reaching consequences. "One word has made a life: one word has marred a life. One word has shaped the destinies of empires and altered the course of history." This is certainly true with some of the words Jesus uttered. When He entered the anxious home of Jairus, it was with the single, simple, yet all-commanding word, "Arise!" that He raised the little girl and evicted death from the house of life and love. "Down the Christian ages like some sound of solemn music in a vast cathedral the Spirit and the Bride are saying, Come!"

The Sixth Word of Jesus on the cross, "It is finished" has been called with perfect justice. It is not only the most general and comprehensive of the seven utterances from the cross, but the greatest, most momentous word in the history of human language and the most wonderful proclamation ever to fall upon human ears since the beginning of the world. If, in the first three cries of the cross we have the *sympathy* of Jesus, and in the fourth and fifth cries His *suffering*, in the sixth and seventh cries we have His *satisfaction*. Of the sixth it is probably true to say that more has been written about it than all the other Words put together.

Yet in spite of all that has been said about this single utterance of Jesus, expositors and preachers return to it again and again trying to plumb its depths. Eternity alone, however, will suffice to comprehend the dimensions of this mighty shout of triumph which Jesus uttered before He died. His proud pronouncement—"finished!"—was like the sound of a heavenly-jubilee trumpet, announcing to heaven, earth, and hell that His death was the conclusion of His mediatorial work; that henceforth there would be peace with God for all who repent through His blood. From John's record of the last words of Jesus, it would seem as if "finished" was the final one He uttered, for after doing so, "He bowed his head and gave up the ghost." But, as we shall discover in our next chapter, Luke recites, "Father, into thy hands I commend my spirit." Yet there is no contradiction here: "We must suppose that what we call the Sixth Word was the ejaculation which accompanied the act of dying, a prayer which concerned the soul of the Saviour and the Father alone. In any case, the words *It is finished* can be regarded as last words in a significant sense. They are the last words which have any reference to the world of men and His business there."

What a contrast there is between the previous saying of Jesus, "I thirst," and the one before us, "Finished!" The former, as we have seen, was a cry of physical suffering and weakness, but the latter was the triumphant cry of spiritual and eternal satisfaction and one which silenced the exultant glee of His foes and the hosts of evil who rejoiced as they watched Jesus die, thinking that would be the end of Him. Having done to death God's dear Son, doubtless His enemies felt they were conquerors at last. That mighty cry of victory ringing out from His dying lips, however, proved Him to be, not a victim, but a glorious Victor over the world, the flesh, and the devil. What His crucifiers thought was His *end* was actually a beginning without an end!

Another striking feature of this Sixth Word that, according to both Matthew and Luke, was uttered with a *loud* voice—the tone implying force and intensity. This was no whisper of dying breath or a word uttered with a murmuring or muttering tongue. The message was strongly audible and doubtless startled those who heard it. John says it was after Jesus received the vinegar, that He said, "It is finished!" That refreshing drink moistened His parched throat, enabling Him with clarity and power to declare His word of consummation. Thus, "that kindly act of the soldier enabled Him to proclaim His victory." Further, it was necessary to make such an announcement of release as loudly as possible so that three worlds could know of the perfect and final work of the cross.

Heaven rejoiced as the loud cry rang through its high arches and many mansions. The angels and the faithful like Abraham who, in faith, saw Christ's triumphant end, lifted up their voices and sang, "Lift up your heads, O ye gates, and the King of Glory shall come in."

Hell trembled as it heard the mighty voice cry, "Finished!" The vaults of the lost world, into which mercy cannot enter, reverberated with a paean of victory. By His death Jesus had destroyed him that had the power of death, that is, the devil. And in the cry "Finished!" the devil must have heard the message of his own defeat and doom. At last, he is a conquered foe.

Earth, for almost two millenniums now, has wonderfully benefited through the finished work of Calvary. "Finished!" —what a cry of hope and inspiration that was in the ears of a devil-ridden and sin-stricken world. The race of Adam, long under the curse, received the joyful news that a full and free salvation had been provided for all under condemnation. So, as one writer summarizes the far-reaching cry:

> *Finished!* That shout rang back against the current of time to the beginning of man's transgression and provided the means of cancellation of transgression for every penitent soul. That shout ran forward to the end of the ages, declaring the fact of salvation accomplished for every believer. That shout ascended to the throne of God, and gladdened the heart of the Father and of the angels; that shout descended to the spirits of men in prison, and prepared them for the moment approaching when He should lead captivity captive, and give gifts unto men.

ONE WORD

All expositors of Scripture point out that the three words as found in the AV, "It is finished," are like the previous cry, "I thirst," only a single word in the Greek, namely, the somewhat lengthy word, *Tetelestai.* This wonderful, victorious word means, "a thing matured" . . . "it is complete" . . .

"it is accomplished" . . . "a task brought to perfection." Its
use by Jesus signified the full accomplishment of His divine
mission as He drank the last drop in His bitter cup and paid
the last farthing of a lost world's debt. This grand and glorious word in the perfect tense declared the completion of the
plan of man's salvation conceived by the mind of God in a
past eternity. *Tetelestai* or "Finished!" is indeed the greatest
single word ever uttered, and may be said "to comprehend in
itself the salvation of the world; and thousands of human
souls, in the agony of conviction or in the crisis of death,
have laid hold of it as the drowning sailor grasps the life-
buoy."

This single word, with its striking grandeur, occurs twice
within three verses. In his introduction to the Fifth Word,
John wrote, "Jesus knowing that all things were now accomplished" or "finished," as it is in the original. The word is
sometimes translated, "fulfilled," an aspect that was in the
Savior's mind at the beginning of His Passion, "This that is
written must yet be accomplished in me" (Luke 22:37). The
fulfillment of God's purpose revealed in prophecy was the
"end" He referred to. We find the same expressive word used
again in reference to the suffering of Jesus by the writer of
Hebrews: "The captain of their salvation perfect through
sufferings. . . And being made perfect, he became the au-
thor of eternal salvation . . ." (2:10; 5:9. See also Luke
24:44, "must be fulfilled").

In Hebrews "perfect" is the same word in the original for
"complete" or "finished." The work of Jesus was to usher in
God's kingdom, but it was equally to complete Himself, to
become perfect and finished, "The finally adequate Revealer
of the Love of God. And this perfecting of the Person of
Jesus was an integral part of the setting up of the Kingdom.
. . . Now as Son of God, He stands forth complete, having
manifested to the full the Divine life."

It is interesting to compare the three times in Scripture
that "God is represented as pausing after bringing the great
district of His work to a conclusion." Such a trio of divine ac-
complishments form a threefold cord that cannot be broken

At the beginning, God, looking upon His new creation of

the universe, rested from all His works because "the heavens and the earth were *finished,* and all the host of them" (Gen. 2:1–3). He spoke, and it was done.

At the midpoint of the world, the center of history, when He who made the world was crucified, He brought into being a new creation, His redeemed Church, with the edict, "Finished." The Chief Cornerstone of heaven was then laid.

At the passing of the old creation, and the bringing in of the new heavens and the new earth, the Creator-Redeemer throned in Glory cries, "It is done," "Finished" (Rev. 21:6. See also 10:7; 16:17). Time is over, eternity has begun.

The Double End

The context does not tell us what was finished when the neuter pronoun is used, *"It* is finished." But what exactly was the nature of the accomplishment expressed? Was the Savior's loud cry associated with the agony of crucifixion, and did He feel the imminent end of His long contest with pain and shame was reached? Doubtless Jesus is brought wonderfully close to us as we realize that His great word of triumph was partly the sense of relief after so much physical and mental suffering. Without question, there was the throb of profound relief in His cry, seeing that His life as the Man of Sorrows was at an end.

While, however, there is no clearly defined statement of what was finished, John would be cognizant of what Jesus had said to the twelve disciples about the accomplishment of those specific prophecies the Son of Man referred to (Luke 18:31. See 22:37). As to whether He had in mind the end of all His anguish or the consummation of a God-given task, James Stalker suggests that the cry, "Finished," was a mixture of both:

> Both the suffering of our Lord and His work were finished together; and it is natural to suppose that He was referring to both. Suffering and service are the two sides of every life, the one predominating in some cases and the other in others. In the experience of Jesus both were prominent. He had a great work to accomplish, and He suffered greatly in the process of achieving it. But now both have been brought to a successful

close; and this is what the Sixth Word expresses. It is, therefore, first, the Worker's Cry of Achievement; and, secondly, the Sufferer's Cry of Relief.

All who went to the place called Calvary "to see the end" must have been relieved when all the malice, enmity, pain, and sorrow were over, for one meaning of "Finished" is "through with, set aside forever." But with their weary sigh of relief that the darkest chapter in world history was over, those onlookers failed to discern that His cry of alleviation was also the shout of triumph and conquest, comprehending within itself the perfect salvation for a sinning world.

It might have appeared to His foes that the life of Jesus had been a failure, seeing He was dying as a malefactor on a wooden gibbet. But when, with a loud voice, He cried, "Finished!" He entered upon a ministry which will follow Him through all the glorious ages of eternity.

Our Lord's own illustration of satisfaction out of and after suffering is that of a woman's travail with the end of her suffering not being a negative cessation from pain only, but an achievement of life, a coming to the beginning of a great joy, wherein she remembers no more the anguish as she fondles her newborn child. It is in this sense of a wider meaning of Christ's cry that John would have us understand by his, *Tetelestai!* On this one word hangs all "the exceeding and eternal weight of glory," as it tells us that all the requirements of the past are fulfilled in it—all the promises of the future depend upon it. Says Steer, "This *Finished* of the consummating and consummated Christ includes in itself all the glories which should follow, with all the sufferings that should go before." Summed up in His marvelous shout was the work of a lifetime and the longings of eternity. No wonder earth heard and rejoiced; hell heard and trembled; heaven heard and sang hymns of praise! Jesus knew that all things concerning reconciliation with God "were now accomplished, that the Scripture might be fulfilled" (John 19:28). The soul of His suffering was the suffering of His soul, for which travail He is now satisfied. Ever bent on doing the will of God who had sent Him into the world to die as the sinner's substitute, by one great crowning act, Jesus opened up the way into the holiest of all. "But not until the end of time itself will that cry yield up all that it contains, for this one great word, *Tetelestai!* served to stake His claim to what we now call the finished work of Christ."

In His High Priestly prayer, Jesus not only anticipated His completed task but spoke of it as if it had already been accomplished, "I have finished the work which thou gavest me to do," which must be understood by the other sentence in the verse, "I have glorified thee on the earth" (John 17:4). As Ellicott comments, "The former sentence is explained by the latter. God was glorified in the completion of the Messianic work of Christ. For this conception of the work of life includes the whole life as manifesting God to man." In His incarnation, Jesus brought God to man, but through His crucifixion He brought man to God. It has been said that if we would win our battles we must fight them as Jesus did *at long range.* "The battle of the Cross was fought and won under the shade of the olive trees in Gethsemane." This was why He could use the past tense in His intercessory prayer, "I have finished the work thou gavest me to do."

THE RENT VEIL

Of all the miracles that took place at Calvary, none is so full of spiritual significance as the rending of the temple veil during the three hours of darkness. Matthew and Mark say that it was "rent in twain from the top to the bottom" (Matt. 27:51; Mark 15:38), and Luke wrote that it was "rent in the midst" (23:45). The veil in question was the inner veil of the temple, separating the two compartments, the Holy Place and the Holy of Holies. Josephus, the Jewish historian, says that it was some sixty feet in length and was hung from four pillars of gilded acacia wood and that the fabric itself was of fine twined linen, covered with richly embroidered cherubim.

The remarkable feature of this mysterious incident is that the veil was not rent by human hands. Of its own accord it became divided in two from the top to the bottom. From "the top" implies that a divine hand tore it in two. Like every other episode connected with the great tragedy of Calvary, the rending of the veil carries a rich, symbolic implication, as the writer of *Hebrews* clearly proves when he deals with the typical aspects of the tabernacle and its services (Heb. 9). The beautiful second veil portrayed the complex personality of Jesus in which heaven and earth were interwoven as warp and woof—the attributes of Godhood being combined with the perfect graces of manhood in an absolute harmony of moral beauty. At Calvary, Jesus was "rent in the midst," or from "top to bottom," and through this divine rending, He accomplished our redemption. Now, we have boldness to enter into the holiest of all by the blood of Jesus; by a new and living way which He has consecrated for us through the veil, that is to say, His flesh (see Heb. 10:19, 20).

On that Paschal Friday, the 15th of Nisan, as the high priest entered the temple at eventide to attend to his customary duty, he was amazed when he saw the inner veil, "The Veil of Separation," ripped assunder from top to bottom as if deliberately torn from above by an unseen hand. How horrified he must have been to witness the destruction of that most holy veil. What are some of the truths signified by the rending of the veil which occurred as the Great High Priest reached the climax of His vicarious pain, bearing on His loving heart the burden of the world's sin, until, passing through hell's door on our behalf, He cried, "Eli, Eli, lama sabachthani"?

THE REVELATION OF THE ANCIENT MYSTERY

Writing of his preaching of the gospel of redeeming love and grace, Paul says of it, it was ". . . the revelation of the mystery, which was kept secret since the world began, But now is made manifest . . ." (Romans 16:25, 26). In his letter to the Ephesians, Paul refers to the specific manifestation he received, ". . . by revelation he made known unto me the mystery . . . Which in other ages was not made known unto the sons of men" (Eph. 3:3–5). Then Paul speaks of himself as a minister of ". . . the mystery which hath been hid from ages and from generations, but now is made manifest to his saints: To whom God would make known what is the riches of the glory of this mystery among the Gentiles; which is Christ in you, the hope of glory" (Col. 1:26–27). Then, in writing to Timothy Paul had this to say, "Who hath saved us . . . not according to our works, but according to his own purpose and grace, which was given us in Christ Jesus, before the world began, but is now made manifest by the appearing of our Saviour Jesus Christ, who hath abolished death, and hath brought life and immortality to light . . ." (2 Tim. 1:9–10).

As soon as our first parents sinned, there came the first prophecy and promise of Calvary in which God dimly announced the coming of His Son, who, after being born of a woman, would suffer vicariously in expiation of sin: The seed of woman shall bruise the serpent's head, and it shall bruise his heel (see Gen. 3:15). That Jesus would come into the world was no mystery then. The mystery was that He was virtually sacrificed before the world began, seeing that when He did appear, it was as the Lamb slain *before* the foundation of the world. Before the disease of sin overtook God's original creation, He had provided the remedy. The constitution of His body, the Church, made up only of those redeemed by His precious blood, was "the mystery hid from the foundation of the world." But that Love drew salvation's plan in a past eternity is now an open secret. Thus the rending of the veil was the complement of the death cry, "It is finished!" The mystery within the Holiest of All was then revealed.

The dying word, *Tetelestai!* takes us back to the first word to leave Jesus' lips, which has been preserved for us, "Wist ye not that I must be about my Father's business?" What was the nature of this business He knew about even at the early age of twelve and which occupied His thoughts? Was it not the program the Trinity sketched out beforehand and which Jesus completed on the cross? On earth, His meat was "to do the will of him that sent me and to finish his work" prescribed for Him in the dateless past.

THE CONSUMMATION OF JUDAISM

Both the tabernacle and the temple with their furnishings and ceremonies were wholly Jewish, but the rending of the veil symbolized their end. When He began His ministry, Jesus said, "Think not that I am come to destroy the law, or the prophets: I am not come to destroy, but to fulfil" (Matt. 5:17). And not one jot or tittle passed from the law until all was fulfilled when Jesus cried, "Finished!" Paul, Hebrew of the Hebrews, made it clear that all law observances were abolished in, and by, Christ when He blotted out the handwriting of ordinances that was against us, which was contrary to us, "nailing it to his cross" (Col. 2:14). The Apostle also reminds us that the law was a schoolmaster leading to Christ, and that once He accomplished His heaven-assigned task, the schoolmaster was no longer necessary.

Not only were all types, symbols, prophecies, and promises of Christ which are found in the Old Testament finished in Him on the cross, but also all the sacrifices of the old Jewish law were then abolished as well as explained. The sacrifice of Jesus not only transcends the lambs slain on Jewish altars aforetime, it superseded them and made them obsolete. ". . . Sacrifice and offering thou wouldest not, but a body hast thou prepared me. . . . He taketh away the first, that He may establish the second. By the which will we are sanctified through the offering of the body of Jesus Christ once *for all*" (Heb. 10:5–10). And the sacrifice on the cross is solitary, sufficient, and supreme because the blood shed was not of a man only—*it was the blood of God,* the purchase price of His Church (Acts 20:28).

Foregleams of redemption were a reality when Jesus cried "Finished!" "From the first gleam of hope in Genesis to the last word of grace in Malachi, every detail foretold and foreshadowed of the life and death of Jesus the Christ had come to pass." All lamps helping to light the way to Him, once His blood was shed, were extinguished. Did He not say that He came as "the light of the world"? Thus, in the broken heart of Jesus, the heart of the Old Testament, so dear to Him, was gloriously fulfilled. This is one reason why the Psalms were so precious to Him. The twenty-second Psalm, for instance, with its prophecy that one consequence of Calvary would be that of condemned sinners regarded as holy before God, without any infringement of His justice, holiness, and truth, was fulfilled by the accomplishment of the suffering Savior. The last verse of this Psalm reads, "They shall come, and shall declare his righteousness unto a people that shall be born, that he hath done this"—"Finished."

The Messianic Psalms, with their depths of desolation and humiliation, were to Him terrible and exquisite anticipations of His approaching death.

Paul declared that "Christ is the end of the law" (Rom. 10:4). All things which the law *required* were "finished" by Him in the life He lived among men. He "fulfilled all righteousness." The old economy was a dispensation of shadows, but with the rising of the Sun of Righteousness it is noontide. In, and by, Jesus, the Ceremonial Law was fulfilled and abolished. When He, as the Lamb of God, was offered up once and for all, Jewish ritual ceased and the condemnation a broken law demanded was cancelled. When the veil was rent in two, altars were overthrown. The great High Priest was about to enter the true Holy of Holies with His own efficacious blood. God's moral law was not made void by the death of the cross. Jesus established this law, given to man in Eden and engraved by the finger of God in clear lines on the human conscience, and then republished it on Mount Sinai on tables of stone. By His death, Jesus honored and ratified this law which is perpetuated in Glory. Now, a lost sinner is saved, not by obeying the law but by divine grace. Jesus performed all the precepts of the law and paid the penalty of the broken law. The cross was "the end of the age" when Christ appeared to put away sin (Heb. 9:26). It was also the end of the law for righteousness to every one that believeth; for by Christ's death, the law could be satisfied (Rom. 10:4). The law says *do*—the gospel cries, *done!* The covenant was ratified and made doubly sure when "the blood of Christ's heart bespattered the divine roll. Then it could never be reversed, nor could one of its ordinances be broken nor one of its stipulations fail."

To write thus about the cessation of the Judaistic order of things in no way suggests contempt for ancient venerable rites. There are those critics of Scripture who affirm belief in the New Testament but dispense with the Old Testament as if it was now of no import. But the Old is the foundation of the New, and both together make one Holy Book. There is no antagonism between the two halves of Scripture. The moral law, being written in the constitution of man, abides forever; but the ceremonial law was designed for temporary use. It passed away by reason of its fulfillment in Christ.

> 'Tis finish'd—Legal worship ends,
>   And Gospel ages run;
> All old things now are pass'd away,
>   And a new World begun.

THE OPEN WAY FOR A LOST WORLD

Further, those outstretched arms, the rent veil, and the triumphant shout enforce the gracious invitation of Jesus, "Him that cometh to me I will in no wise cast out" (John 6:37). Through the cross, the way into the holiest is open to all who are willing to repent of their sin and believe the gospel. No priest can interpose between the soul and God. All is done that could be done for the sinner's reconciliation to God. A lost world's everlasting freedom was purchased by the sacrifice of Christ who, when He cried, "Finished!" pronounced the death-knell of sin's dominion and brought complete deliverance to the door of every man. As the *Te Deum* expresses it, "When Thou hadst overcome the sharpness of death, Thou didst open the Kingdom of Heaven to all believers." Sin's thraldom was crushed and broken by a death that was:

Voluntary. Some time before He died Jesus said, "I lay down my life that I might take it again. No man taketh it from me, but I lay it down of myself. I have power to lay it down, and I have power to take it again." Then, referring to the marring of His body at Calvary, He declared, "Destroy this temple, and in three days I will raise it up. . . . He spake of the temple of his body." Thus His life on earth, His

death, and His resurrection were wholly voluntary. He rose
from the dead because it was not possible for Him to be
holden of death. The life of Jesus, then, was not *taken,* but
given.

Vicarious. Paul pressed the gospel into a nutshell when he
wrote, "Christ died for the ungodly." It was because God
loved "a world of sinners lost and ruined by the Fall," that
He gave His only begotten Son to die for their salvation.
Jesus "had to press His weight against the huge iron gates of
human guilt and doom and force them open." When He had
done so, He cried, "It is finished!" Now His message to mankind is clear and plain: "Behold, I have set before you an
open door, and no man can shut it."

Victorious. Jesus was the only man who could pass judgment upon His life's mission. We often say of a person when
death or retirement compel cessation of labor, "Well, his
life's work is finished," by which we mean ended, and that
opportunities for making it more complete are over. When
we have done the best we were able to do, we must still say,
"We are unprofitable servants." Only the Perfect Man could
say of His task, "It is perfect; it is flawlessly complete"—
which is what the triumphant *Tetelestai!* implies.

The impressive feature of such perfect achievement is that
of its accomplishment at an early age, for Jesus was not an
old decrepit man when He cried "Finished!" He was only
thirty-three years of age when his life's work was ended—
the age when for most of us life is only beginning. In the
eighth century poem, *The Dream of the Rood,* we have this
sentence, "Then the *young hero* begirt Himself—that was
God Almighty and strong and stern-minded; He ascended
the high gallows, brave in the sight of many, when He
would set mankind free."

With us, it is a mystery when a young life, after years of
education and careful preparation, suddenly comes to the
end of the road with all hopes of the future blasted. But the
death of "the young Prince of Glory" teaches us that it is not
the length of a life that counts, but the quality of it. Alas! too
many live long lives without any conception of God's will
and purpose for life. Whether we die young or old matters

little if we have lived in the will of God, for only then can we die content that His purpose for our life is finished.

As we take a last look at this Sixth window through which we can see a victorious Savior, it may prove helpful to briefly summarize the ingredients in the remedy He provided for a sinful and sinning world. It was Bengel who remarked that, "They are many voices making up one symphony"; and all Seven Words sing in a sevenfold chord the nature and cost of our redemption. So let us go over the constituent elements in the achievement of the cross.

Tetelestai proclaims the *manifestation of the love of God.* It was because God loved us that He "sent His Son to be the propitiation for our sins" (1 John 4:10). The word in the Greek for "propitiation" is akin to the one used for "mercyseat" in Hebrews 9:5—Jesus became our mercyseat sprinkled with His own blood. At Calvary we have the evidence that God loved the world, for in His crucified Son we see "the love of God's heart, and the heart of God's love," in a most revealing way. The measurement of the heart of God is infinite, "As far as the east is from the west, so far hath he removed our transgressions from us" (Ps. 103:12). Start walking from the east and walk on forever and you will never reach the west. That little word of two letters in John 3:16, "God *so* loved the world," indicates that His eternal love found its supreme expression in His grace as manifested on Calvary. That *so* is vast enough to girdle a sin-stricken world and bind it back to God. The rent veil inspires our redeemed hearts to sing:

> For the love of God is broader
> Than the measure of man's mind;
> And the heart of the Eternal
> Is most wonderfully kind.

Tetelestai proclaims the *vindication of the justice of God.* All claims of divine justice were satisfied when Jesus cried "Finished!" Justice demanded death for sin, and Jesus discharged the debt. Because God remained just, He is now the Justifier of all who believe in His Son who suffered the penalty of man's disobedience to divine law. As Spurgeon so forcibly expresses it:

> The great ten-thonged whip of the Law was worn out upon His back; there is no lash left with which to smite one for whom Jesus died. The great cannonade of God's Justice has exhausted all its ammunition; there is nothing left to be hurled against a child of God. Sheathed is Thy sword, O Justice! Silenced is Thy thunder, O Law! There remains nothing now of all the griefs, and pains, and agonies which chosen sinners ought to have suffered for their sins, for Christ has endured all for His own beloved, and *It is finished.*

Tetelestai proclaims the *complete conquest of satanic forces.* Does not your heart thrill whenever you read Paul's remarkable tribute to the accomplishment of Christ when He died in our place? Here is what he wrote to the Colossians: "Having cancelled out the certificate of debt consisting of decrees against us and which was hostile to us: and He has taken it out of the way, having nailed it to the Cross. When He had disarmed—or divested Himself of—the rulers and authorities, He made a public display of them, having triumphed over them through the Cross" (Col. 2:14–15, NASB).

Because of the glorious victory of the blood-bespattered Gladiator in the arena of Calvary, He is now "Head over all rule and authority" (Col. 2:9. See 1 Cor. 15:24). Because Satan fell from his heavenly abode like lightning, the saints now have authority over all the power of the enemy (Luke 10:18). As the ruler of this world, Satan was cast out by Jesus (John 12:31), who now has freedom from his approach (John 14:30). Satan has been judged and condemned (John 16:11), and he is a defeated foe over whom we have victory through the cross (1 Cor. 15:57).

The double purpose of the life and death of Jesus is stated by John in clear and simple terms: ". . . he was manifested to take away our sins; and in him is no sin. . . . For this purpose the Son of God was manifested, that he might destroy the works of the devil" (1 John 3:5, 8. See Heb. 2:14). When in his own life's blood, Jesus wrote *Finis* to the dominion of satanic powers, having destroyed the authority of Satan, He was able to emancipate those held captive by sin.

The rent veil proclaimed the end Daniel foretold when He wrote, "To finish transgression, and to make an end of sins, and to make reconciliation for iniquity, and to seal up vision and prophecy, and to anoint the most holy." Now, sin need not have any dominion over us. Freed from sin as a master, and now servants to God, we have fruit "unto holiness, and the end everlasting life" (Rom. 6:22). Before He was born, the name chosen for Him was Jesus, seeing He came to save from sin. And by His cross He furnished and finished a perfect salvation for men—not only salvation from the penalty and guilt of sin for sinners, but salvation from sin's power and government for all who are saved by grace through faith in Him.

Tetelestai proclaims the *provision of grace and glory*. All man needs as a sinner, here and now, and then as a saved sinner, hereafter, was fully and perfectly provided through the rent veil of the Redeemer's flesh, as the various rich and expressive evangelical terms declare.

There is the "robe of righteousness" with which we are covered (Isa. 22:21; 61:10). Self-righteousness is a filthy garment. No merit of our own can be placed upon God's altar. "The Lord is our Righteousness." Unless clothed in divine righteousness or justified by grace, we cannot stand before Him. Says Robert Gilchrist:

> This righteousness is a robe, of which Christ's passive obedience is the warp, and His active obedience the woof. It is flowered all over with the Christian graces. The finished robe is the perfection, and it is now ready to be put on with a view to the marriage supper of the Lamb. "By the obedience of One shall many be made righteous." . . . The finished righteousness of Christ is of inestimable value. . . . It is the most precious treasure a man can possess.

Paul declares that when Jesus became the propitiation for our sins, He demonstrated God's righteousness by which He can be just, yet the justifier of all who believe in Jesus (Rom. 3:25, 26). Because we are made righteous by the blood of the Righteous One, it is our responsibility to live righteously, that is, to have the right spirit in all that concerns us. Christ *for* us, must become Christ *in* us. If the first aspect is perfect, the second must ever be imperfect, as the grand proposition of Augustine states:

> Between the righteousness which justifies and the righteousness wrought in us by that justification there is all the width of difference between the immortal and mortal, the Divine and the human, the perfect and the imperfect.

Tetelestai proclaims *there is the acquisition of atonement.* Paul affirms that it is through the death of Jesus that we have received the atonement (Rom. 5:10–11). Some translators give us "reconciliation," which is what atonement actually is. Once enemies of God, we are now reconciled to Him as the result of Christ's finished work. To *atone* is easily understood if you make the one word two, *at one.* Root meanings of *atonement* imply to expiate, to effect reconciliation, to cause to be friendly. To be reconciled to God means that we are *at one* with him or at peace with Him, through the blood of His cross upon which He became our Peace-Offering. A finished work of reconciliation was necessary to win for outcasts the right of access into God's presence, and this Jesus provided by the rent veil of His flesh

The fact that Jesus, at His ascension, entered heaven itself to appear before God for us is proof of the finished character of the atonement (Heb. 9:24). All who were afar off are assured of an everlasting reconciliation with the Father. Now, no suffering of man can be added to His complete atonement. As believers, we may suffer—and do—but our sufferings are disciplinary, not propitiatory. They are the chastisement of a Father, not the infliction of a Judge. As the Lamb, Jesus was provided by God to expiate and remove sin, to reconcile us to God, to honor divine government, and presenting to God an infinite atonement through His blood, He cried, "It is finished." In his *The Cruciality of the Cross,* Principal Forsyth has this comment:

> Today it may be more needful in certain positions to preach the Christ of the Cross than the Cross of Christ. There is a

strategy in the holy war. It is the last crisis that calls reserves to the front. But whether we preach the Christ Who atoned or the atonement of Christ, it is still an atoning Christ and an atoning Cross we preach.

Paul's one object of his faith and the one theme of his preaching was not Christ Himself, but Christ crucified. He cannot be severed from all His cross provided when He gave Himself without limit to recover us from all sin and bring us to God. Does Jesus not bear the marks of His conflict in His glorified body?

Tetelestai proclaims *there is the blood-bought redemption.* What a glorious gospel the crimson word "redemption" proclaims! *Tetelestai!* meant the fulfillment of all Old Testament types and prophecies of deliverance from sin through the sacrifice of One who had no need of redemption. Dr. C. I. Scofield tells us that the word itself means "to deliver by paying a price" and gives us the following comment, "The completed truth is set forth in the three words which are translated redemption:

"*Agorazo*—'to purchase in the market.' The underlying thought is of a slave market. The subjects of redemption are 'sold under sin' (Rom. 7:14), but are moreover under sentence of death (Ezek. 18:4; John 3:18, 19; Rom. 3:19; Gal. 3:10), and the purchase price is the blood of the Redeemer who dies in their stead (Gal. 3:13; 2 Cor. 5:11; 1 Pet. 1:18).

"*Exagorazo*—'to buy out of the market.' The redeemed are never again to be exposed to sale.

"*Lutruo*—'to loose, to set free by paying a price' (John 8:32; Gal. 4:5, 31; 5:13; Rom. 8:21)."

Redemption is by sacrifice and by power (Exod. 14:30). Christ paid the price, the Holy Spirit makes deliverance actual in experience (Rom. 8:2). The shout of triumph, "Finished," means that the cross will ever remain the source and symbol of our transcendent redemption accomplished "once for all." Having paid the full price of our emancipation from sin's slavery, there can be no further propitiation for sin. Lange, the renowned commentator, says of Christ's Sixth Word:

Finished was His holy life; with His life, the struggle; with His struggle, His work; with His work, the redemption; with the redemption, the foundation of a new world.

Inbred and practiced sin exposed men to guilt and judgment and made them captives in the stronghold of death, but Jesus stormed this dread stronghold and paid the ransom to set them free from sin and death (Heb. 9:27–28; 10:12). Once released from such bondage, as those bought with a price, they are sanctified through the same offering of the body of Jesus Christ once for all (Heb. 10:10). Redeemed by blood, we have the Redeemer as our inheritance with His power to support us, His wisdom to guide us, His love to comfort us, His mercy to relieve us, His goodness to supply us, His justice to defend us, His covenant to secure us, and at last, His heaven to receive us.

> 'Tis finish'd—the Messiah dies
> For sins, but not His own;
> The great redemption is complete,
> And Satan's power o'erthrown.
>
> 'Tis finish'd—All His groans are past:
> His blood, His pains, and toils,
> Have fully vanquished our foes,
> And crown'd Him with their spoils.

Tetelestai proclaims *there is the hope of Glory.* The cross not only provided our salvation from sin's dominion, here and now, but safety forevermore. Golgotha opened a door into Glory for all who accept Jesus as their Savior. Apart from the vast angelic host in heaven, the only other occupants are those washed in the blood of the Lamb (Rev. 7:14). The work achieved at Calvary included all the glories which should follow. Not only were all the requirements of the past fulfilled when the veil was rent, all the promises of the future were assured, for on the one word, *Tetelestia!* hangs all "the exceeding and eternal weight of glory." What treasures of hope lie concealed for the redeemed in the shout of the dying Redeemer, who will not be fully satisfied with all His travail of soul until His Church, purchased with His own blood, is complete and with Him in Glory!

Jesus laid the foundation of His Church at Calvary. He had promised that He would build her on all He is in Himself, and thus His cross and His coming are united. "Christ was once offered to bear the sins of many; and unto them that look for him shall he appear the second time without sin unto salvation" (Heb. 9:28; 1 John 3:2, 3). When He returns for His own, as He said He would, then His spiritual temple will be finished to the topmost spire, and from the heavenly throne will ring the glorious fiat, "It is done!" (Rev. 16:17; 21:5). During the hours of darkness when the veil of the temple was rent in twain, Jesus, by His sacrificial and triumphant love, secured for us the threefold salvation Paul sets forth in his masterly Epistle to the *Romans*.

1. Past Salvation. The Apostle affirms that ". . . the gospel of Christ . . . is the power of God unto salvation to every one that believeth" (Rom. 1:16). Once a sinner repents and accepts the Savior, who died and rose again that there might be a gospel to believe, he is immediately saved from the *penalty* and *guilt* of his sinful past. All previous sins are blotted out and remembered no more against the sinner. So in testimony meetings happy hearts bless God for the day when their hearts were made clean. But delivered from all transgressions committed in our Christless days, the Lord does not leave us saying, "I have saved you, now try to keep yourself saved. I have wiped the slate clean, don't incur any more debts." Bless Him, by His shed blood, Jesus made provision for our present as well as our past.

2. Present Salvation. Having received Jesus as our Savior from all past guilt, we walk in Him, experiencing a day by day salvation from the *power* and *government* of sin. We were delivered from its thraldom, and thus sin need not have any further dominion over us. The tragedy is that far too many of us confess to having been saved, but we are not being saved. Paul has a striking passage in which he emphasizes this double salvation. Twice over he uses the expressive phrase *Much more!* "But God commendeth his love toward us, in that, while we were yet sinners, Christ died for us.

Much more then, being *now* justified by his blood, *we shall be* saved from wrath through him. For if, when we were enemies, *we were reconciled* to God by the death of his Son, *much more . . . we shall be saved* by his life" (Rom. 5:8–10).

Here, then, is a twofold salvation finished at Calvary—a salvation from our past sinful and estranged condition, and a daily salvation from Satan and sin, as well as from the wrath of God in the future. *Much more,* being reconciled to God! Can there be much more—more than the blessed reconciliation effected when we believed? Paul says there is, for we are not only saved by Jesus' death, but by His life. "We shall be saved by His life." *His life?* What phase of His life? Surely not His life before His death, although it was such a holy life. Trying to live like Jesus cannot save a sinner from his guilt. There is no salvation by imitation.

Paul did not have in mind the *past* life of Jesus, but His *present* risen, glorified, throne-life. Because He who died to save us from our sins, rose again, and is alive forevermore. He is able to save us to the uttermost, seeing He ever liveth to make intercession for us (Heb. 7:25). Victory over all the wiles of the devil to rob us of the joy and the assurance of salvation is ours through Jesus Christ, the Living One. "I am Thine, save me" (Ps. 119:94).

> Jesus is stronger than Satan and sin,
>   Satan to Jesus must bow;
> Therefore I triumph without and within;
>   Jesus saves me *now.*

3. Prospective Salvation. Although saved from our sinful past by the blood of the cross and kept saved by the dual intercession of Jesus and the Holy Spirit, we still live in a sinful world and are subject to the temptations of the devil who is its god. What we must have, then, is the final installment of the salvation purchased at Calvary, namely, our complete salvation from the entire *presence* of sin. It is this phase of redemption which draweth nigh that Paul had before him when he wrote about the day being at hand,

". . . knowing the time, that now it is high time to awake out of sleep; for now is our salvation nearer than when we believed" (Rom. 13:11).

Did we not receive salvation when we first believed? Yes! Do we not experience a full salvation as we keep on believing? Yes! Then what aspect of salvation is this that is *nearer* than the moment of our initial faith in the Redeemer? Is it not the full result of salvation which shall be ours when we are caught up out of a sin-cursed world to meet the Lord in the air? Then, and not till then, we shall be saved to sin no more. Not until Jesus appears for us shall we be perfectly like Him—sinless! (1 John 3:2). What a blessed hope; we shall be changed into his likeness!

> *Dying* with Jesus, by death reckon'd mine;
> *Living* with Jesus, a new life divine;
> *Looking* for Jesus till glory doth shine,
> Moment by moment, O Lord, I am Thine.

Hubert Simpson in his *Testament of Love* describes a picture painted for the Royal Corps of Signallers depicting an incident during World War II. A signaller had been sent out to repair a cable snapped by shell fire and was shot while trying to restore the interrupted contact. The picture shows him lying dead in the fulfillment of his task, holding together the broken ends—holding them in contact. Beneath the picture is the one word, "Through!" Then Dr. Simpson goes on to make this application of the artist's great painting:

This is what Christ did for us by His death. Sin had snapped the contact between God and man. The Divine current was interrupted. Alone, in No-man's-land, unarmed save with infinite understanding and infinite love Christ brought the broken ends together in His death. For this had He come into the world, to restore the interrupted communion. He established contact in His death. Beneath the Cross of Calvary we write the one word—*Through!* In Him contact with God is reestablished and made sure, and by the answering voice of pardon that meets our cry of need, we know that we are *through*.

By His death, resurrection, and ascension Jesus became the one and only mediator between God and men, and no man can get through to the Father but by Him. This is why the New Testament enumerates the manifold blessings we now have *through* our Lord Jesus Christ as the result of His finished work. Apart from Him, we have nothing, can do nothing, and are nothing. He is above all, through all, and in all. Through all He accomplished by the pain and anguish of the cross we are:

Through from our sin to His righteousness and salvation.
Through from our failure and defeat to Calvary's victory.
Through from the weariness of fight to infinite resources of heavenly power.
Through from death to live evermore.
Through from mortality and time to eternity.

A final word remains to be said about the Savior's shout of achievement, "It is finished!" His completed work for us should be a mighty motive to us to strive to finish some task for Him. It was the great aim of Paul to end his course with joy, "I have fought a good fight, I have finished my course, I have kept the faith" (2 Tim. 4:7).

When Jesus said that it was His meat to do the will of Him that sent Him and to *finish His work,* He left us an example that we should follow His steps. How apt are the lines of Gambold:

Perhaps for His name, poor dust I am,
Some work I shall finish with glad loving aim,
I still—which is best—shall on His dear breast,
As at the beginning, find pardon and rest.

But is it our daily endeavor to bring our whole life under the discipline and directing force of the inspiration of Jesus' cry as he hung upon the cross? If we believe that God has a plan for our life, are we determined to be faithful unto death in the realization of such a plan? Is there the great unifying principle in our lives for which everything else makes way? "With God there is finality," as the triumphant

Tetelestia proves. Is the passion of finality ours, enabling us to say at the end of the day, "I have finished the work thou gavest me to do"? We have to confess that too often we are like the man in the parable that Jesus spoke about who "began to build, but was not able to finish." There are too many stops and starts on our pilgrimage. "In form, the Jewish Bible, unlike the Christian, has no climax; *it stops, ours ends.* This is the difference between the earthly work of our Savior, and all other lives, *Finished!* No one has ever been able to say that but Jesus."

When Cecil Rhodes, who wrote his name across a continent, was heard to murmur as he came to die, "So little done; so much to do." While, no matter how diligent and faithful we may be, our task will never be perfect as was the Savior's, yet if we are faithful unto death, living for God and serving Him to the limit of our capacity, reward will be ours. If we live for the Lord and die in Him, our works go with us into the presence of the Lord, and receive His benediction (Rev. 14:13). Whatever we do, if it is for the glory of God, it will return with satisfaction, earning for us the Savior's word of blessing, "Well done, good and faithful servant, enter thou into the joy of thy Lord."

The Seventh Word of Love

LOVE THAT SURRENDERS

*" 'Father, into Thy hands I commit My spirit.'
And having said this, He breathed His last"*
Luke 23:46, NASB

Love That Surrenders

A conspicuous feature of pure love is its willingness to surrender itself to the object of affection or the glad sublimation to the care and confidence of the one loved. Beholding the rich young ruler, Jesus loved him, and asked for the full committal of his life and possessions, but was refused. All too glibly we sing,

> All to Jesus I surrender,
> All to Him I freely give.

Love never seeks its own, never fails. No matter what love may give up, it is never impoverished. How eloquent of this attractive facet of love Calvary is! In His last word from the cross Jesus is found committing himself unreservedly to His heavenly Father, as He passes out of time into eternity. Having taught men the art of living, Jesus now exhibits the art of dying in the full assurance that God would keep throughout eternity what He was entrusting to His Father.

Throughout the previous meditations we have been actually watching a death bed. But now all the pain and anguish are over and peace and stillness will prevail, and we wait for the final word. Before he expires, the dying One speaks. His previous saying, "It is finished," was His farewell to earth. His last word, "Father, into thy hands I commend my spirit," was His entrance greeting to the world beyond the present vale of tears.

IT WAS THE LAST WORD

As we have already seen, the first three Words on the cross were spoken at intervals during the initial sufferings of Jesus. Then there came the three hours of darkness at the conclusion of which Jesus gave utterance to His cry of forsakenness. But with all darkness and mystery passed, the last three Words followed in rapid succession. The truth that "every work of God delays at first, and hastens at the end" is apparent with the progress of the Seven Words, the last of which was a fitting climax to the whole. It was a grand consummation of these Calvary communications, proving that never man spake like Christ Jesus. This is the reason why we should listen intently to His last words.

While all the words Jesus uttered in the days of His flesh are full of interest and instruction, His *last* word has special importance attached to it and claims our particular attention. Usually, it is difficult to catch the farewell word of a loved one dying, perhaps, in a semi-consciousness state. If it is intelligently uttered, usually it is in a very low, soft voice those at the bedside must strain to hear. But there was no tired whimper in the last committal of Jesus. His brief prayer was not uttered in weakness but "with a loud voice." That strong voice declared the last assertion of His royal power to make the free and full disposal of His spirit.

The last word from the cross reminds us of the sevenfold completeness of the Seven Words as a whole. Apart from the Fourth Word, no Evangelist gives all seven. Matthew and Mark give one only, Luke gives three, and John gives three. Thus, here, as elsewhere, Bengel's expressive principle applies: "the four books are four voices which conjointly make

up one symphony." Number seven has ever been associated
with perfection and completeness, and to the Jewish mind
the seven utterances from the cross indicated a consummation comparable to the seven days of creation. "The redemptive work of Christ has reached its climax in the Sixth
Cry, and the Seventh Cry breathes the spirit of rest and
resignation. The loud cry in which the Son of Man has
proclaimed His finished work was followed in rapid sequence by the words with which He faced the approach of
death."

IT WAS A QUOTATION FROM SCRIPTURE

As all the Old Testament was full of Jesus, which He
Himself affirmed when He said of the Scriptures, these "are
they which testify of me" (John 5:39), so He was full of the
Scriptures even as He hung upon the cross. Truly, no word
can adorn the lips of a dying man as the Word of God. Jesus
lived in the Scriptures and honored them by quoting from
them in His final moments. The law of the Lord was the
home of His spirit, the rule of His practice, and His comfort
as He died. "It is strange," says one writer, "that He should
need to quote Scripture. We might have thought He could
dispense with that and have used His own words."

Because Jesus knew where to go to, in the only part of the
Bible He had, for the language He needed for His own heart
and for the guidance of others, it was most fitting that He
should find His final word in David's great Messianic Psalm:
"Into thine hand I commit my spirit: thou hast redeemed
me, O Lord God of truth" (Ps. 31:5).

In the dying Savior's use of this verse we have an addition
and an omission. As yet God was not known to the Jewish
nation as a whole as "Father." So David did not employ it
but gave in its place the title, "Lord God of truth." Then
the omission, "For thou hast redeemed me," was apt, for the
sinless One had no need of redemption. It would be unfitting
for Jesus to use the words of Himself seeing He was dying
as the Redeemer of a lost world. Perhaps He finished the
verse in the ears of God only, "I have redeemed *them*."
Jesus, then, took the words David employed in a season of

great distress and robed them with a new and richer content than when they were first penned.

IT WAS A PRAYER

The shout of triumph, "Finished!" merges into the prayer of peace and assurance, "Father, into thy hands." Scripture was turned into prayer, and the most effective prayers are those saturated with the truths of Holy Writ. Prayer was the habit of our Lord's life. The Gospels reveal a prayer life of constant, unbroken communion with His Father. Prayer had been the language of life for Jesus, and so His latest breath is a prayer, indicating that such a ruling passion was as strong in death. Prayer is the most appropriate exercise for dying persons, but some will only come naturally if theirs has been the habit of praying through life. Out of the Seven Words *three* were prayers, namely, the First, Fourth, and Seventh Words. James Stalker, writing on the final word of the cross being a prayer, says:

> Praying was distinctly the language of His dying hours. It was not by chance that His very last word was a prayer, for the currents within Him were all flowing Godwards.

The two personal prayers beginning and ending the Cries of the Cross were petitions already consecrated by the devotion of many centuries. Prayer for forgiveness of sin; prayer of an assured blissful immortality. A death bed without a prayer, a word of Scripture, a testimony on the lips, any recognition of God, or of any hope beyond the grave is a sad sight to behold. If our last end is to be like the Savior's, who died the death of a righteous man, then our life must be righteous. If we live without God, and die without Him, what a terrible afterlife will be ours!

IT WAS A WORD TEACHING US HOW TO DIE WELL

It is recorded of a noted saint that, when on his death bed, he said to a relative, "Come near and see how a Christian can die." As we meditate upon the death of Jesus, His last word especially teaches us how to die. It also contains the art of living as well as the art of dying. The one art influences and shapes the other. It would seem as if the closing moments of the life of Jesus were an invitation to come and see how a crucified Man could die. He never had the solace of privacy as He died. His death was a public spectacle for men and angels to witness, and what a wonderful departure from this life they witnessed—a life of holy living climaxed by holy dying. In a somewhat interesting volume of mine, *Last Words of Saints and Sinners,* which can be used as a companion work to the present one on *Seven Words of Love,* there is a chapter devoted to "The Art of Dying Well." Here the treatise is developed that too little is said or written about the graceful art of folding up our earthly tent, and the art of dying along with the art of living are the least learned of all arts. Are we among the fully prepared who can subscribe to the lines?

> I want, and this sums up my prayer,
> To glorify Thee till I die.
> Then calmly yield up my soul to Thy care,
> And breathe out in Faith my last sigh.

If we love and serve the Savior, then death will be no leap in the dark for us. Living in eternity's sunrise, ours will be no fear when death, the king of terrors, calls us from earth. Faber has it, "Trust in God is the last of all things and the whole of all things." Jesus certainly exhibited this axiom in life and death. David said, "Mark the perfect man . . . for the end of that man is peace" (Ps. 37:37). It was so with the only perfect Man who ever lived, whose end was not only serene and confident, but precious in the sight of His Father into whose hands the Son surrendered His spirit in the confidence of a glorious immortality.

A few hours before his sudden death, Matthew Arnold worshiped in the Sefton Park Presbyterian Church, Liverpool, England, and the last hymn the worshipers sang was this:

> When I survey the wondrous Cross
> On which the Prince of Glory died

My richest gain I count but loss,
And pour contempt on all my pride.

Reaching home from church, Arnold repeated these lines and uttered his conviction to friends that this is the greatest hymn in our language. "Yes," Arnold went on to say, "the Cross remaineth, and in the straits of the soul makes its ancient appeal." That very afternoon he passed in a twinkling out of the shadows into the light eternal. We can only hope that the famous poet's soul was ready to meet the Savior who, as He died upon the cross, died well because He had lived in the orbit of God's will.

A SACRED RELATIONSHIP—FATHER!

Coming to a more intimate examination of this last word from the cross, we cannot but be impressed with the affirmation of an eternal relationship existing between Father and Son. It is no accident that the First Word and the Last Word commence with the filial term "Father." Jesus entered the darkness of the cross with the word upon His lips, and when He reached the climax of all His suffering, and accomplished our redemption, it is into His Father's hands that He commits His spirit. The double use of "Father" implies absolute unity of spirit and purpose between God and His only-begotten Son and wonderful confidence of complete filial trust.

Having come down from God, the first word Jesus learned to frame in His infancy was *Abba* or "Father." At an early age He asserted His Sonship and His obedience when He said that He was in the world to do his Father's business (Luke 2:49). When Jesus entered His public ministry, the Jews sought to kill Him because of His claim that God was His Father, thereby making Himself equal with God, which He was! (John 5:18; 10:29–30). He was a loving Son to the last for He "became obedient unto death, even the death of the cross" (Phil. 2:8). We may recall Della Robbia's *Crucifixion* housed in the Duomo at Areggo, in which the artist has not hesitated to represent the figure of the Father's face above the cross, bending over His Son with an expression of deepest compassion, yet of content over his obedience. At Calvary we see the heart of the child loving the Father and fulfilling His wishes.

There was not only separation of time between the First and Last Words, which were two prayers, each commencing with "Father," but also a whole world of anguish and sorrow. If, during the three hours of darkness, Jesus seemed to lose the sense of His Father's presence, yet He still clung to Him and died with the sweet and tender word "Father" on His lips—evidence of a heart at rest on His mighty bosom. As Jesus breathed His last, He was confident that He was going home to His Father. Having known Him from a past eternity, God, to him, was not a blind and unknown force, but His "God and Father." Thus, always conscious of the presence and nearness and love of His heavenly Father, it was only natural that as He died, He knew His Father's arms were around Him. His last word was like that of a weary child calling, "Carry me, Father," upstairs.—*Into thy hands* I commit my spirit. Krummacher remarks that

> All the thoughts and deeds, desires and efforts of Jesus tended toward His Father and the glorifying of His Name. To accomplish His Father's will, was His meat and drink; the love of His Father His delight and bliss; and union with Him the summit of all His hopes and desires. . . . We must still regard the words *Father into Thy hands I commit My spirit,* as the War-Cry of a Warrior engaged in battle. Hell, which raged around Him, did not give up its cause as lost, but continued to assault Him in every way, and to distress Him; and the act of death cost Him, Who was Life, no small effort.

We die well if we die conscious that we, too, are the sons of God, and that our reliance upon God, as our heavenly Father, will bring us peace of heart, even as it did his Son. Did not Jesus Himself teach us to look up to God and address Him as "Our Father who is in heaven"? And has not God, through grace, sent the Spirit of His Son into our hearts enabling us to cry, "Abba, Father" (Gal. 4:6)? The same Father, who was near to His Son in the hour of His grief, watches over us with the same tenderness of love. In the

hour of our trial and suffering do we have the same trustful
confidence in our Father above as Jesus had? With the
precious word "Father" ever on His lips, Jesus moved among
men and taught them how to live.

The poet William Canton draws the picture of his little
girl coming to say "Good night" to him, bringing her play-
things with which she has finished for another day, for him
to lay by:

> When she stands between my knees
> To kiss good-night, she does not sob in sorrow,
>   "Oh, father, do not break or injure these,"
> She knows that I shall fondly lay them by
> For happiness to-morrow
> So leaves them trustfully.
>   And shall not I?
>
> Whatever darkness gather
>   O'er coverlet or pall,
> Since Thou art Abba, Father,
>   Why should I fear at all?

A Safe Refuge—Into Thy Hands!

From the moment God sent His Son to earth to effect the
sinner's reconciliation with Him, His soul was never, not
even for a moment, out of the Father's keeping. And your
soul, and mine, are never out of the Father's power and
providence. Is this not the truth Jesus taught when He spoke
to His disciples about *the double grip?* "My sheep hear my
voice, and I know them, and they follow me: And I give
unto them eternal life; and they shall never perish, neither
shall any man pluck them *out of my hand.* . . . No man is
able to pluck them *out of my Father's hand.* I and my Father
are one" (John 10:27–30).

Yet although the hand of God was ever upon His beloved
Son, it was by God's determinate counsel and foreknowledge
that by "wicked hands Jesus was crucified and slain." But at
the last, with clean hands, He went from men's wicked hands
into His Father's hands. He had been betrayed into the
hands of sinners (Matt. 17:22, 23; Mark 14:41; Acts 2:23),

but now the blessedness is His of falling into the hands of His loving Father. We are warned that if we die in sin it is a fearful thing to fall into the hands of a living God (Heb. 10:31). Jesus, however, was no unrepentant sinner caught up at last by the hands of a righteous sin-hating God, but rather a loving and obedient Son around whom were the everlasting arms of the Father He ever pleased.

The phrase "Into thy hands" quoted from the ancient Psalm implies not only the returned sense of the Father's presence after the cry of desolation, but a testimony to the world that He had overcome the sharpness of death *before* He died. Moffat translates this last utterance, "Father, I trust My Spirit to Thy hands." As a child falls asleep in his father's arms, so Jesus passed away in the clearest consciousness and with fuller confidence that He was departing to be with His Father, which was far better. To the Son, the Father's hands were the synonym for safety, strength, security, and supreme satisfaction. The question is: Are we found following the example of Jesus in committing all that concerns us to the power and tenderness of God's gentle hands, yet hands able to subdue all things to Himself?

Can we say that we are daily learning how to leave all the intricate affairs of life safely and confidently in the hands of God that opened heaven to His beloved Son, and through Him to all believers? Those mighty hands are the executants of divine love and wisdom, as well as of justice, and are the only safe refuge for all who are harassed by anxiety. Those hands that fed the sparrows assure me that their Possessor cares for me. David was not walking in obedience to God when he wrote, "Let us fall into the hands of the Lord, for His mercies are great." But as His saints, we are already in those hands and none can pluck us out (Deut. 33:3).

> Our times are in Thy hand:
>   O God, we wish them there;
> Our lives, our souls, our all, we leave
>   Entirely to Thy care.
>
> Our times are in Thy hand;
>   Jesus, the Crucified.

Whose hand our many sins have pierced,
Is now our guard and guide.

A Sublime Resignation—I Commit My Spirit!

Weymouth's translation of these last words of Jesus reads, "Father, to Thy hands I entrust my spirit." The word "commend" the AV gives us means "to lay down" or to surrender or resign, and implies that Jesus Himself had finally decided the precise moment when He would go to His Father in Heaven. Thus, "His death was His last act." Death did not take Him by surprise, for He knew, where, how, and when He would lay down His life, and after death, take it up again. Jesus did not die as we die. Life did not leave Him as it leaves us. We know not the exact hour of our departure. But when the Savior said, "I commend my spirit," He used words signifying the sovereign assertion of His power of control, and that by the free and active choice of His own will, He would *lay down* His life as the Good Shepherd for His sheep.

Archbishop Loane points out that the word "commend" which Jesus used finds an echo in the participle used by Paul in a significant passage: "I know whom I have believed, and am persuaded that he is able to keep that which I have *committed* unto him against that day" (2 Tim. 1:12). "Jesus would leave His spirit as a trust in the hands of His Father just as Paul would commit himself to Him in whom he had believed. He knew God would keep that trust as a deposit is kept in its place of custody against that day when it would be required. Then it would be restored when the crisis of death was past and He possessed His body and spirit once more in the glory of His resurrection."

What was the nature of the treasure Jesus deposited with His Father? It was His *spirit*. Alas! man takes such pains with his *body*, to feed and care for it and maintain it in life and vigor, but he is criminally negligent about his *spirit*. Yet this is the very thing he should be solicitous about, seeing it is the last charge he commits to God. In the Gospels, *spirit* and *soul* are used as identical terms, and Jesus is said to have had both (Matt. 26:38; 27:50; John 12:27; 13:21;

19:30; Isa. 53:12). But God is spoken of as the Father, not of *souls* but of *spirits* (Heb. 12:9). The *body* of Jesus was committed to Joseph of Arimathaea for burial, but His *spirit* was deposited with God who, as a perfect Trustee, guarded it until the treasure was returned.

The *spirit* is the highest, most sacred part of our being. It is "the most lofty and exquisite part of the inner man," says James Stalker. "It is to the rest of our nature what the flower is to the plant or what the pearl is to the shell. It is that within us which is specially allied to God and Eternity." C. H. Spurgeon, Prince of Preachers, has the comment:

> Our spirit is the noblest part of our being; our body is only the husk, our spirit is the living kernel, so let us put it into God's keeping.

When Jesus prayed of resigning His *spirit*, He was not referring to the Holy Spirit, but to His own human spirit, which was ever moved with compassion for the perishing, and was ever full of sympathy for the sick and sorrowing. With the believer, committal of the spirit in the hour of death is the personal, unhesitating surrender of "that part of his sanctified nature which is peculiarly superhuman and clings most closely to the Father, Whose dearest possession on earth it is." So, trustfully, Jesus deposited His life with Him who is the Father of life, the great Fountain of spiritual existence, and who is, in Himself, God the Spirit.

In the days of His flesh Jesus had taught that His Father was not the God of the dead but the "God of the living." His last word from the cross, then, was proof of immortality and that death would not destroy His flawless life. The deposit He made was likewise a pledge of resurrection, just as the body of every believer is buried "in sure and certain hope of resurrection." To quote Stalker again:

> Jesus knew that He was launching into Eternity; and, plucking His spirit away from those hostile hands which were eager to seize it, He placed it in the hands of God. There it was safe. Strong and secure are the hands of the Eternal. They are soft and loving too. With what a passion of tenderness must

they have received the spirit of Jesus. "I have covered thee," said God to His servant in an ancient prophecy, "in the shadow of My hand," and now Jesus, escaping from all the enemies, visible and invisible by whom He was beset, sought the fulfilment of this prophecy.

In life and in death we should be found committing the keeping of our souls to God in well doing, as unto a faithful Creator (1 Peter 4:19). Grace should be ours, not only to resign our spirits to God's safekeeping but to all that concerns our pilgrimage of life. We should commit ourselves to His grace, to be daily saved by it; to His power, to be daily kept by it; to His providence, to be daily fed by it; to His care, to be daily preserved by it; and to His arms at death, to be safely landed in His august presence above. If we are found living in the will of God, death will not come to us as a tyrant. "How strange this fear of death is!" George Macdonald once exclaimed to a friend, "Yet we are never frightened at a sunset." As with Jesus, so with ourselves, death will be a glorious sunset and the dawning of a more blessed day in summerland where eyes are never wet with the tears of separation.

> Hide me, O my Saviour, hide,
>   Till the storm of life be past:
>   Safe into the haven guide;
>   Oh receive my soul at last.

A Sweet Repose

Luke records that Jesus after uttering His final word on the cross, "gave up the ghost" (23:46). Matthew puts it, "Jesus, when he had cried with a loud voice, yielded up the ghost" (27:50). Then Mark, in similar language says, "Jesus . . . gave up the ghost" (15:37). John's precious addition is, "He bowed his head, and gave up the ghost" (19:30). In each case, the meaning is that Jesus dismissed, or resigned His spirit, and that the dismissal of His spirit was an act of His own will; that by His own volition His redemptive work was finished and therefore qualified Him to ascend up where He was before His incarnation (John 6:62).

The action of Jesus, then, was both a command and a committal. When Moses and Elijah came down from heaven to the mount, it was to talk with Jesus, not about His death outside the city wall of Jerusalem, but of His *decease,* or *exodus,* or going out, into death, and through it, emerging as the One alive forevermore. Thus, His last act was His exodus, accomplished in the so-called Holy City (Luke 9:31). The same word the Gospels used for the expiration of Jesus is the one Paul employs to describe the Father's action in yielding up His Son to die for our salvation. "He that spared not His own Son, but *delivered Him up* for us all, how shall He not with Him also freely give us all things?" As the Father willingly delivered up His Son, so the Son voluntarily surrenders His spirit in accordance with the everlasting covenant.

Among the various translations of our Lord's final announcement and action my personal preference is for that given by the *New American Standard Bible:* "Father, *Into Thy Hands I Commit My Spirit.* And having said this, He breathed His last" (Luke 23:46). How suggestive are these four words, "He breathed His last!" Such a final breath was the final evidence of His humanity, for as the eternal, pre-existent One, it was impossible for Him to draw a last breath. But when He entered the body prepared for Him, He had to suffer its limitations, even to its appointment to die once. Thus, as the Son of Man, He breathed His last. But is it not blessed to know that

> Our blest Redeemer ere He breathed
> His tender, last farewell,
> A Guide, a Comforter bequeath'd
> With us to dwell.

When Stephen, the first martyr of Christianity, was being stoned to death, his end closely resembled the Master's going out. Like Him whom Stephen loved, he repeated the first prayer of Jesus on the cross for His enemies, "Lord, lay not this sin to their charge." Then he imitated Jesus' last prayer in slightly different form, "Lord Jesus, receive my spirit." Stephen addressed to Jesus the dying prayer He Himself had offered to the Father. "With all that clearness of mind and freshness of intellect, and fluency of words that might have been possible to Jesus," says Spurgeon, "He did not invent a new sentence, but He went to the Book of Psalms, and took from the Holy Spirit this expression, *Into thy hands I commit my spirit.*" And this borrowed, dying word summed up the principle on which Jesus had always lived.

As in His living, so in His dying, Jesus set an example so many of His followers have emulated, beginning with Stephen, who was the first to catch the same spirit of love and used the same language as his Master in the hour of death. The last word from the cross was also the dying words of saints like Polycarp, Jerome, Basil, Bernard, Columbus, Martin Luther, and Melanchthon. When John Huss was being led to execution, callous priests in derision stuck on his head a paper cap scrawled over with pictures of devils to whom they had consigned his soul. But again and again Huss cried, "Into thy hands, O Lord, I commend my spirit!" It was the same with Latimer and Ridley, bound back to back at the stake at which they were to die in Oxford. Latimer, aged, frail, and worn was seen to bathe his hands in the fire; then he died, almost without a pang, crying, "O Father in heaven, receive my soul." Ridley suffered longer and more painfully but was heard to utter as he tasted the dark waters of death a similar prayer to that of his companion in martyrdom.

When, where, and how we may meet death is mercifully hid from us. The certainty is that, if we are not alive when Jesus returns for His own, as He said He would, then we must go home to heaven by the way of a grave, as Jesus Himself did. But if we are among His redeemed ones, then we have no reason to be afraid to die. The thought of death is the best motive for a holy life, and a holy life is the best preparation for death. The most effective rehearsal for death is the awakening every morning to a fresh consciousness of our heavenly Father's love and protection, and that nobody and nothing can pluck us out of His hands. Then, when the end comes, whether we are young or old, meet death naturally or tragically, conscious or otherwise, we shall still be in God's safe-keeping, as we pass over the great divide. What better staff could we have to lean on as we breast the river of death than, "Father, into thy hands I commend my spirit." Who could wish his spirit to be carried away to God in a more glorious chariot than that which the last prayer of Jesus provides? If we habitually trust ourselves in Christ's hands for life and death, for time and eternity, our dying cry will only crown the acts of our life.

If we desire our last words to be words of prayer, we must learn to pray always with all prayer and supplication in the Spirit. If we would have the Father's face smile upon us as we die, we must, in life, acquaint ourselves with Him and be at peace. If, as we gaze upon the dying Savior or think of dying saints and of their last message, and say, "Let me die the death of the righteous, and let my last end be like his," we must experience what it is to be clothed with His righteousness, live the life of the righteous, and practice all the requirements of such a virtue. When Rowland Hill, the stirring revivalist preacher and hymnist came to die in 1833, he was heard to repeat the lines he himself had written:

> And when I'm to die
> Receive me, I'll cry;
> For Jesus hath loved me,
> I cannot tell why.

BIBLIOGRAPHY

Preachers and students desiring a more intensive study of the Seven Words of the Cross can find rich devotional material in the many commentaries covering the Gospels. Albert Barnes' *Notes on the New Testament* (Grand Rapids, Mich.: Kregal); Matthew Henry's *Commentary on the Whole Bible* (Old Tappan, N.J.: Revell); *Critical and Explanatory Commentary on the Whole Bible* by Jamieson, Fausset, and Brown (Grand Rapids, Mich.: Zondervan Publishing House); Charles J. Ellicott, editor, *Ellicott's Commentary on the Whole Bible* (Grand Rapids, Mich.: Zondervan Publishing House); *Dictionary of the Gospels*, edited by James Hastings, are just a few that could be consulted with profit.

Then it will be usually found that all volumes dealing with the work of the cross, such as James Stalker's most illuminating and penetrating study, *The Trial and Death of Jesus Christ* (Grand Rapids, Mich.: Zondervan Publishing House), have sections devoted to Jesus' Seven Words. F. W. Krummacher's large volume, *The Suffering Saviour* (Chicago: Moody Press) is another work of the same order, as is *The Radiant Cross* by Paul S. Rees. Mention can also be made of *The Wondrous Cross,* by David James Burrell, and of *Verbum Crucis,* by William Alexander, Bishop of Armagh.

The following works are exclusively occupied with Christ's messages from the cross.

Dickie, E. P. *Seven Words from the Cross.* London: Arthur H. Stockwell.

167

Fraser, Neil K. *The Grandeur of Golgotha.* London: Pickering and Inglis; Neptune, N. J.: Loizeaux Brothers.

Gilchrist, Robert. *Christ Lifted Up.* London: Marshall, Morgan and Scott.

Good Friday: A Manual for Clergy. London: S.P.C.K.

Loane, Marcus L. *The Voice of the Cross.* London: Marshall, Morgan and Scott; Grand Rapids, Mich.: Zondervan Publishing House.

Lockyer, Herbert. *The Lenten Sourcebook.* Grand Rapids, Mich.: Zondervan Publishing House.

Matthews, Dean W. R. *Seven Words.* London: Hodder and Stoughton.

Mortimer, Alfred G. *Meditations on the Passion.* London and New York: Longmans.

Randolph, B. W. *The Example of the Passion.* London and New York: Longmans.

Reid, S. J. *The Seven Windows.* Grand Rapids, Mich.: Wm. B. Eerdmans Publishing Co.

Simpson, Hubert L. *Testament of Love.* London: Hodder and Stoughton.

Spurgeon, C. H. *Christ's Words from the Cross.* Grand Rapids, Mich.: Zondervan Publishing House.

Tucker, Paul. *Christ's Words from the Cross.* London: Evangelical Press.

Unknown Christian. *The Gospel from the Cross.* London: Marshall, Morgan and Scott.